ESSENTIAL SAILING

ESSENTIAL
SAILING

ROGER MARSHALL

The Lyons Press

Copyright © 2000 by Roger Marshall

Printed in Canada

First edition

Designed by PageMasters & Company

10   9   8   7   6   5   4   3   2   1

Library of Congress Cataloging-in-Publication Data
Marshall, Roger.
    Essentail sailing / Roger Marshall. —1st Lyons Press ed.
      p. cm.
    ISBN 1-55821-771-1
    1. Sailing. I. Title.
GV811.M258   2000
797.1—dc21   99-27140
                                 CIP

CONTENTS

INTRODUCTION

Many years ago I was standing on a dock getting ready to go on an ocean race. Another sailboat was moored near our stern, and the skipper was looking rather anxious. He asked me if I knew anybody who could replace him on the crew for the race. I suggested he call Keith Ludlow, a college friend of mine. Keith had learned to sail in a campus program and had no offshore racing experience, but he had been my crew while sailing dinghies. At the time Keith was a newcomer to the sport of sailing. Yet from that first offshore race, Keith went on to become the rating coordinator for the Royal Ocean Racing Club in England. He traveled worldwide as a respected member of the Offshore Racing Council and sailed on many boats throughout the British Isles.

Sailing took Keith around the world, just as it has for me. I have sailed in every ocean except the Arctic, as well as in the Mediterranean Sea, the Baltic Sea, the English Channel, and the Irish Sea; in San Francisco Bay, in Perth, Australia, and in the lake above the Nairobi Dam in Kenya. One recent trip was a transatlantic crossing from New York to Falmouth, England, aboard a hundred-foot sloop. You too can travel to many places, whether it is across the Chesapeake Bay, a short cruise to the San Juan Islands, or around the world to visit foreign lands. A sailboat can take you there using the most natural force in the world—the wind.

But traveling is only part of the mystique of sailing. There's also the camaraderie. A boat can be a microcosm of the world. Sailors tend to be interesting people because they've often sailed to exotic places. They've sampled new cuisines, and seem to have a lively interest in learning more about their environment and the places they visit. Sharing a boat, I believe, gives you a better chance to get to know people than any other sport offers. This is part of what makes sailing such a voyage of discovery.

The first step on this journey is learning to sail. And learning to sail takes commitment: You won't master it in one day or even one week. You might figure out how to handle a boat and operate its sails in a one- or two-week sailing program, but that is only a beginning. You'll find that you'll learn more about sailing every time you go out in a boat. I still discover something new every time I sail, and I have been doing it for more than forty years. Learning is one of the greatest rewards of sailing: finding out more about the sport, yourself, and the people and places around you.

This book is a start along the sailing journey. You will learn how to handle a boat, how to interpret the wind and tide, what to look for when you buy a boat of your own, and how to navigate a safe passage in that boat. Of course, the information here is fairly brief; it is merely intended to get you started. The complete manual of sailing would be an enormous book—if it could be written at all.

CHAPTER 1

LEARNING THE ROPES

Before you step aboard a boat there are a few essential things you should know. The first is to wear a life jacket at all times. According to U.S. Coast Guard figures for 1996, 446 lives could have been saved had the victims been wearing life jackets. When you learn to sail, you will make mistakes. At one time or another most sailors have ended up in the water. Wearing a life jacket keeps you afloat while you figure out what to do.

If you understand how a boat sails and the purpose of its various lines, the process of learning about sailing will be easier. That is the intent of this book—to help you understand a little about sailboats and how to sail them even before you step aboard.

BORROWING OR BUYING A BOAT

You don't need your own boat to start sailing. One alternative is to go to a sailing school and learn on the school's boats. All the dings and dents you put in the hull by bouncing it against the dock won't be ones that you have to pay to repair. Another option is to sail on a friend's boat for a while before investing in your own boat. Both routes will allow you to acquire some knowledge before you become your own skipper.

WHERE DO YOU FIND A SAILING SCHOOL? Finding the right sailing school can be fairly easy. If you combine learning to sail with a vacation, then your options multiply. Open any phone book to the yellow pages, under SAILING SCHOOLS. If that doesn't work, try calling your local yacht or sailing club. If you still cannot find a sailing school, ask local boatyards or yacht brokers which school they recommend. You can also ask at a local boat show, or at a marina, or even at a sporting goods store that sells sailing gear. Most marinas, yards, and brokerage houses are willing to help— once you learn to sail, you might become a client.

Once you have found a school, don't be intimidated into thinking you must suddenly look and sound like a yachtsman. Far from it. Everybody who is attending the school is a beginner like you, with exactly the same goal: to learn to sail. It matters not what you wear, or what you know. Get out on the water and enjoy it.

If you insist on buying at this early stage, you will learn more, and learn it more quickly, if your first boat is small. Larger boats require more crew, with each person having only one or two jobs to do. On a small one-person boat you are the captain, the mate, the crew, the bottle washer, and everyone else. You alone have to pull in the mainsheet, helm the boat, lower the centerboard, navigate, and trim the sails. This demands that you learn about everything going on around you.

Chapter 11 will outline many of your options for buying boats. I have included information on everything from dinghies to multi-hulled racing boats.

SWIMMING AND SAILING

Many sailors do not know how to swim and simply wear a life jacket all the time. However, it's always worth learning to swim, whether you are five or fifty years old. Most YMCAs offer programs throughout the year; you can learn to swim in the winter and learn to sail in the summer. Being able to swim helps to give you more confidence when moving around on a boat. I recommend that every sailor learn to swim. It will certainly enhance your sailing skills.

I REMEMBER WHEN . . .

When I learned to sail many years ago, it was in a heavy wooden Wayfarer dinghy owned by the local sailing school. Now my children are learning the delights of sailing in Optimist dinghies in a course presented by the local yacht club. Their struggles with the language and terminology of sailing, the vagaries of the wind, and the abilities of their partners bring back my own memories of beginning this sport. I remember the times when I forgot that dinghies continue to turn if you hold the tiller over, making you sail a complete circle, usually to the consternation of the person crewing the boat with you. And I remember capsizing because I inadvertently gibed or tacked the boat before my partner was ready. (Gibing or tacking is when the boat turns so that the wind blows on the other side of the sails. When the bow of the boat passes through the wind, the maneuver is called a tack; when the stern passes through the wind, it's a gibe.)

Of course, I was taught what to do in the event of a capsize, but the memories of the event remain with you for years. In most instances, the boat tips over until the mast is parallel to the water. In some capsizes the boat turns completely upside down. One particularly memorable capsize ended up with me walking around the hull of the boat, standing on the centerboard, and righting the boat without even getting my feet wet. My crew swam around the boat while I stayed dry! Such a feat doesn't endear you to your crew, but at least you can chuckle over it years later.

As my sailing skills advanced and my level of confidence rose, I found myself going farther and farther afield, meeting more people and exploring many new places. The same will probably happen to you when you take up this sport. Maybe you'll sail around the world like many sailors have done. All it takes is that first step: looking for a sailing school or asking a friend to show you how to sail.

HOW A BOAT SAILS

In earliest times, when humans were still clomping around in furs carrying stone clubs, the only means of transportation was by foot. But somewhere along the line an ancient mariner rode a log downstream. Propulsion at that time was supplied by paddling furiously with both feet. The next step in the evolution of a sailboat was for the ancient mariner to hold a large, leafy branch in the air and let the wind propel the log downwind. And the leafy branch eventually evolved into a sail made of skins.

Sticking a sail on a log is a sure way to capsize it, so sails were installed on rafts. Gradually, the raft evolved into a hollowed-out log, and in Polynesia two logs were lashed together to make a catamaran. With a rudder attached, a catamaran could be steered. Long ocean voyages were made in catamarans, but almost always downwind, or slightly across the wind. The sail acts to block the wind and gets dragged downwind. Today, some sails are developed specifically to drag the boat downwind. These sails are called spinnakers and look like a large triangular balloon. In fact, they were originally called balloon spinnakers.

It wasn't until some form of keel in the shape of a centerboard, leeboards or daggerboards were discovered that boats were able to sail against the wind. A leeboard is a narrow board fitted to the hull on the outside of the vessel. It's lowered when the boat needs to sail to windward. Boats have leeboards on both sides of the hull; only the leeward one (downwind) is lowered. A centerboard is similar to a leeboard, but projects out of the bottom of the boat on the centerline. A daggerboard is located on the centerline of the boat and moves vertically up and down like the blade of a dagger. It has its own box and often projects up through a boat's deck. A centerboard is hinged at the front and lifts up into the center of the hull.

To prevent the boat from sinking, a centerboard is contained in its own box. Leeboards, daggerboards, and centerboards can be raised. A keel, on the other hand, is fixed below the boat. Keels are usually constructed of lead to make them heavy and to keep the boat upright. It is the interaction between the water and the keel or centerboard that enables a boat to sail against the wind. Even then, a sailboat cannot sail directly into the wind; the best it can do is to sail at about forty-five degrees from the wind.

Like an airplane wing, sails need to develop lift to enable them to harness the wind. Lift is the force created when an airfoil-shaped sail surface is placed at an angle of incidence to the direction that the wind is coming from. That is, the wind needs to blow across the sail so the sail can work. By setting the sails to resemble an airfoil, you get the most lift from them. This is true whether you are sailing upwind or across the wind. However, it's difficult to set the sails to get lift from them when you sail directly downwind; they work better when blocking the wind. This is why a boat going downwind cannot sail faster than the wind.

TRY THIS EXPERIMENT   When you are a passenger in a car that is going slowly, open the window and hold a piece of cardboard vertically against the wind passing by the car. Feel how hard the wind is blowing against the cardboard. This is what happens when a sailboat is sailing downwind with its sails up.

Now lean the cardboard forward. As it gets closer to the horizontal plane, it will want to lift upward. If you bend the cardboard to make it look like an airplane wing, you can get even more lift from it. Now turn the cardboard so that the front or leading edge is vertical. Lift is generated either toward or away from the car. This is the principle that makes a sail work. Sails are airfoils and must be shaped and positioned at the best angle to the wind direction.

When the wind strikes the sails, it makes the boat want to go sideways and heel over. Without a keel, the force of the wind will simply push the boat sideways. For example, try sailing a dinghy without the centerboard down. The dinghy will move forward because the hull is sailing at a small angle of leeway (angle of incidence), allowing it to generate a small amount of driving force, but you will usually find that the dinghy goes sideways about as fast as it travels forward.

The keel or centerboard counteracts the wind force trying to push the boat sideways. In doing so, it too generates a force. This force can be resolved into two components. One is drag, which is slowing the boat down; the other is the keel side force, which is stopping the boat from sliding sideways. When the forces in the sails (the driving forces) are strong, the boat accelerates until the keel and hull forces (drag and side force) exactly match the driving forces. The boat then sails along with all forces in equilibrium. Gusts in the wind are countered by a touch more heel, a slight movement of the helm, and a slight increase in acceleration until all the forces come back into equilibrium. When these forces are in balance, the boat sails upwind. Figure 1.1 shows the theory in action.

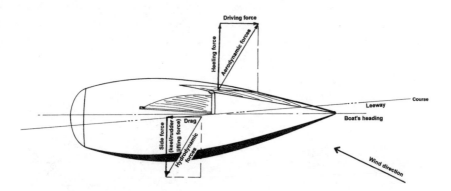

FIGURE 1.1 How the hydrodynamic forces match to the aerodynamic forces. The wind on the sails generates a force that tries to blow the boat to leeward. But one component of this force tries to drive the boat forward, while the other component drives it to leeward. The keel resists sliding to leeward, and as it moves forward, it generates a lifting force. The combination of keel, rudder, and hull in the water produces drag, which tends to slow the boat. When the aerodynamic forces are in balance with the hydrodynamic forces, the boat moves at a steady speed through the water. If the aerodynamic forces increase, the boat accelerates, and if the hydrodynamic forces increase, the boat slows down.

As the boat turns farther away from the wind, the keel plays a smaller and smaller part in the efficiency of the hull. In fact, the keel is not needed when the boat sails directly downwind. It's extra drag and slows the boat. This is why some boats have centerboards, leeboards, or daggerboards that can be raised.

THE WIND

The wind that blows across the water is constantly changing. Sometimes it will gust or lull; other times it might shift one way or another. To sail a boat at its optimum efficiency, a helmsman has to feel the wind movement and turn the helm just enough to counter it to bring the hull and sail forces back into balance. This art is the true skill of the sailor.

If you're a first-time sailor, it may be difficult to figure out how to trim the sails to their optimum, how to keep the boat from tipping over too far, how to helm, and how to feel the wind. Learning all these skills takes practice, lots of it. There are several things you can do to help yourself learn about the wind.

When you are sitting on a seawall, thinking about nothing in particular, look at the surface of the water. Make a note of where the water is fairly smooth. That's where there is a lull in the wind. A dark, rippled patch means that a gust is moving across the water. Watch the gust coming toward you and see if you can feel the increase in wind strength.

If you hold up a short piece of string (about six to eight inches, or 1500 to 2000 mm), known as a telltale, you will be able to tell the wind direction. (Because turbulence comes from your hand and arm when you are holding the string, this experiment will work better if you tie the string to a short stick, like a wand.) Hold this telltale up in front of you and watch how the wind blows it from side to side. This will give you an idea of how much the wind moves around. Also note that the direction the wind is blowing from can affect its gustiness. For example, a cold northerly breeze tends to be gustier than a hazy southerly. (You'll learn more about this in Chapter 10, on weather.)

When you get aboard a boat, you can attach telltales to the shrouds and to the leading edge of your headsail. (All sails set in front of the mast are call headsails. A headsail may be a jib, a genoa, or a topsail.) The very best sailors attach telltales to the trailing edge of the mainsail, too, to show how the wind is blowing over it. By watching these telltales when you are sailing, you will be able to keep the sails working at their best.

When you are out on a boat, you will probably sail close to shore on your first few trips. This means that the wind will bend around other boats, tall buildings, trees, and over land—an effect called turbulence. If you want to see a good example of turbulence, make yourself a tall glass of iced coffee and pour a dash of milk or cream into it. The swirls made by the cream as it moves through the coffee and bends around the ice cubes reveals turbulence. If the ice cubes were tall buildings, the wind would bend around them just like it does in your coffee. A sailor steering a boat must watch out for the effects of turbulence. It can create a sudden gust that heels the boat way over, or it might make the wind come from a different direction and catch the sails from the wrong side. Sailors call this being taken aback—an example of sailing terminology that has become part of everyday language. In other words, the wind is blowing onto the back side of the sail.

Turbulence can be especially strong in areas of high bluffs or buildings. The wind can hit a high building and go around or over the top. As it goes around the building, it's squeezed, and its speed increases. (If you have ever walked between two tall buildings, you may have noticed how the wind seems to be stronger.) Wind may also change its angle. It may be southerly in front and astern of the buildings, but along the east side it may be south-southeast, and on the west, south-southwest. If you stand close to the back of the building, you may feel no wind at all. As you walk downwind away from the building, you will feel the wind gradually increasing. Sailors call this effect being in the lee or in the wind shadow.

Out on the water, wind shadows affect the wind strength and direction. A wind shadow from another boat might last up to twenty boat lengths downwind from that boat. Sailing in that shadow will slow your own boat down. A wind shadow can be caused by land, another sailboat, a tree, a high building, or a bluff upwind of you. If there is high land upwind of you and the wind is blowing over its top, you may find that there is no wind in the lee. If you look at the water under the lee, you will be able to see that it's flat; there is no wind. Usually you can see where the wind starts by looking at the water and noting where small wavelets begin. This is the edge of the wind shadow.

As your skills increase and you begin to race or cruise, you will learn what features will give you an edge, what will slow the boat, and what areas to avoid.

TIDES AND CURRENTS

On a hot summer's day it seems hard to believe that the sea or the water in a lake is moving. In the ocean, the sea is always moving, while a lake may have water flowing in at one end and out at the other. The movement of water is caused by currents and tides. Some currents—such as the Gulf Stream which flows around the north Atlantic—move millions of tons of water a minute. Other currents may move a few gallons of water per day.

Tides are caused by the gravitational pull of the moon. In general high tide occurs every fourteen hours or so, depending on the lunar day. The farther away from the equator you are, the greater the rise and fall of the tide, although the local topography plays some part, too. For example, in Florida you may see a rise and fall in the tide of one or two feet, while in Maine the rise and fall may be fourteen to sixteen feet. In some areas of the world, such as the Bay of Fundy and the Bay of Biscay, tides rise and fall nearly forty feet!

As the water rushes between islands and bridges, you might see some strong currents generated. In a small boat these areas are usually places to avoid. Most dinghies can sail at four to five knots, and larger sailboats can sail faster—some planing boats at up to eighteen or twenty knots. But tidal currents can also run at high speeds. For example, the current at the Race at the end of Long Island Sound can run at four to four and a half knots. Off Alderney, in the English Channel, the Alderney Race may run at speeds up to nine knots.

Tidal currents can be used to your advantage. Suppose you want to go in the same direction as the Race. If the speed of your boat is six knots and the current is four knots, you will be traveling at ten knots. Sailors call this speed over the ground (SOG), and it's different from the boat's speed. If your boat speed is six knots and you are going against the current in the Race, your SOG will only be two knots (6 - 4 = 2).

Beginning sailors are generally taught to sail in areas of low current. But you should be aware of the effects of a tidal current and how they can be used to your advantage. If you must learn how to sail in an area of strong currents, make sure you have a chase boat to tow you home if the wind dies—or else the tide might take you along with it.

THE POINTS OF SAIL

You have learned that a sailboat cannot sail directly into the wind. It must sail at an angle to the wind direction. When a boat is sailing upwind, it's said to be closehauled. Upwind is when the boat is sailing toward the wind with the wind striking the boat anywhere forward of the beam. (Beam is a transverse line across the middle of the boat.) Downwind is when the wind is coming from astern or anywhere aft of the beam.

You need to be able to see where the wind is coming from in order to trim the sails properly. Figure 1.2 shows the various angles of sail. If the boat is not quite closehauled, it's sailing on a close reach (this wind angle may also be called a close fetch). A close reach is anywhere between closehauled and a beam reach. When the wind is abeam—that is, blowing directly across the side of the boat—you are sailing on a beam reach. When the wind is about forty-five degrees aft of the beam, the boat is sailing on a broad reach (or fetch). If the wind is coming directly from astern, the boat is sailing dead downwind or running downwind. This is usually the slowest point of sail. If the wind is coming from directly ahead of the boat, causing the sails to flap and the boat to stop moving, the boat is said to be in irons.

Note that the wind direction shown in Figure 1.2 is the apparent wind angle, which is different from the true wind angle. To tell the difference, imagine yourself in a car on a rainy day. When the car is stationary, the rain is falling straight down. When the car is moving forward, the rain seems as if it is leaning toward you. Actually, it's still falling straight down, but your velocity makes it slope toward you. If you put your hand out the car window, the rain will appear to strike it at an angle that varies with the speed of the car. Wind, although you cannot see it, does the same as shown in Figure 1.3.

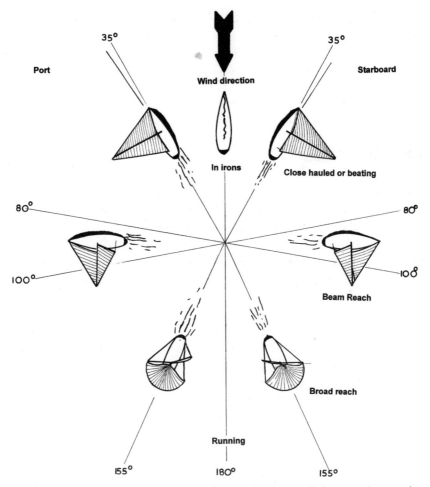

FIGURE 1.2 The various angles of sail. The wind direction here is the apparent wind—that is, the wind you experience when the boat is under sail. True wind is the wind that you feel when you are standing still.

You should also understand the difference between the true and apparent wind speed or wind strength. When the true wind is blowing from the northeast at ten knots, a boat motoring toward the northeast at six knots will see a wind strength of sixteen knots. But a sailboat cannot sail directly into the wind; it must sail at an angle to it. A sailboat heading upwind when the wind is from the northeast will sail almost easterly on one tack and northerly on the

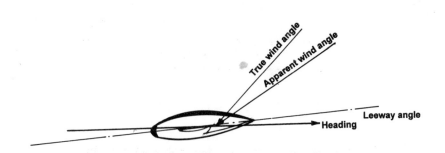

FIGURE 1.3   Apparent/True Wind angle.

other tack, and in both cases its speed will be about six knots. Because the wind speed increases due to the speed of the boat, it will seem as if the wind is blowing from north-northeast or east-northeast at fifteen knots or so. If the same boat under the same northeast wind were to run off to the southwest at six knots, the apparent wind would be four knots $(10 - 6 = 4)$.

CHAPTER 2

GETTING STARTED

Before you get into a boat and sail off over the horizon, you need to learn the names of the major parts of the vessel. It's no use knowing that you must haul on the halyard if you have no idea what a halyard is. In fact, a halyard is the rope used to haul the sails up the mast. The name comes from the days of old sailing ships when a rope was used to haul the yards up the mast, the yards being the crossbars that support the sails. Similarly, you might think that a sheet is a sail because as a kid you may have used a bedsheet as one. But a sheet is actually the rope used to pull the corner of the sail in or out, not the sail itself.

THE LANGUAGE OF SAILING

However you start sailing, among the first things you'll learn are the names of the various parts of the boat. As one sailing instructor put it: "You'll learn the name of the lump of wood on the end of the tiller." She didn't say which end of the tiller she meant.

Sailing is replete with terms derived from non-nautical language. For example, a sail has a head, a foot, and a belly. The hull

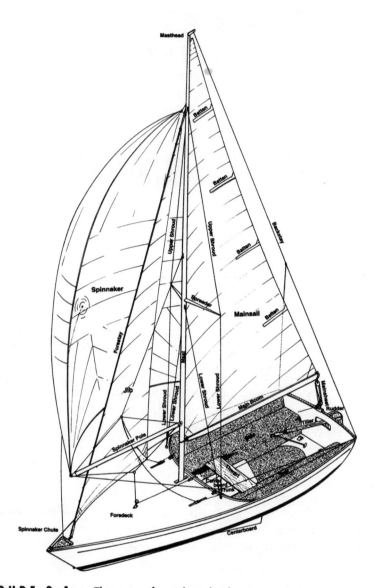

Labels on figure: Masthead, Batten, Batten, Upper Shroud, Upper Shroud, Backstay, Batten, Spreader, Spinnaker, Batten, Mainsail, Batten, Forestay, Mast, Mainsheet, Rudder, Jib, Lower Shroud, Lower Shroud, Lower Shroud, Main Boom, Tiller, Spinnaker Pole, Center Board Trunk, Foredeck, Spinnaker Chute, Centerboard

FIGURE 2.1 The parts of a sailing dinghy. A seat going across the boat is called a thwart, and in this case it's used to steady the centerboard trunk. The centerboard drops out from the bottom of the trunk. The spinnaker pole is held by a bridle on the top and bottom. The lower half of the bridle is the foreguy, while the top half is the topping lift. Note that the jib sheet is led over the pole and the topping lift. When the spinnaker and pole are dropped, the jib is ready. If the jib sheet were led under the pole, it would have to be re-led when the spinnaker was taken down. On this boat the spinnaker is taken down by pulling the line in the center of the sail down through the spinnaker chute.

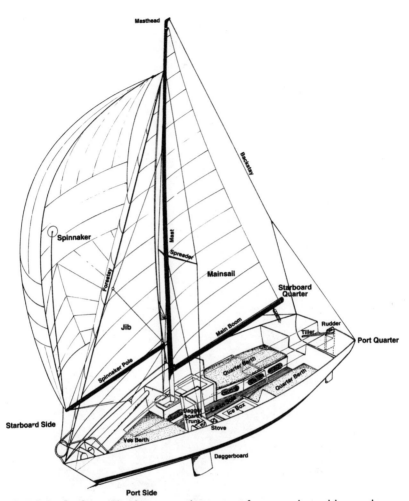

Masthead

Spinnaker

Backstay

Mast

Spreader

Forestay

Mainsail

Starboard
Quarter

Jib

Main Boom

Rudder

Tiller

Port Quarter

Spinnaker Pole

Quarter Berth

Quarter Berth

Starboard Side

Dagger
board
Trunk

Ice Box

Vee Berth

Stove

Daggerboard

Port Side

FIGURE 2.2 This boat can sleep up to four people and has a dagger-board instead of a centerboard or a keel. The simple accommodations include a sink, icebox, lockers for storage, and room for two adults and two children.

of a boat has ribs, knees, and elbows. You also probably take for granted many sayings that have nautical roots. The term *son-of-a-gun* is one example. In olden times the only place for a woman to give birth on the lower deck of a warship was between the guns, and any child born there was known as a son-of-a-gun.

The glossary, beginning on page 177, contains a list of sailing terms that you should learn. In this chapter I'll focus on the ones most often used. These are illustrated in Figures 2.1, 2.2, and 2.3,

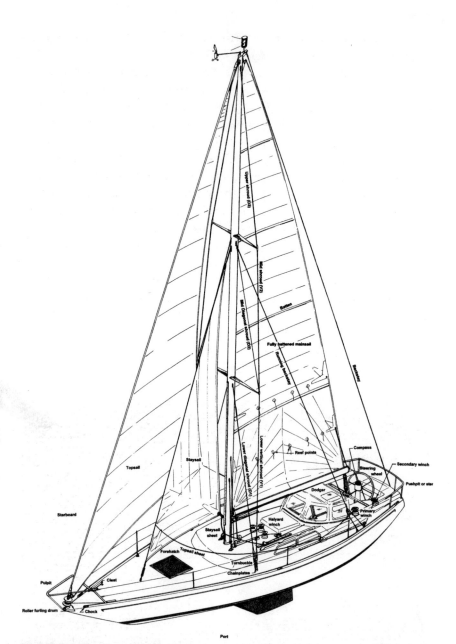

Upper shroud (D3)

Mid shroud (V2)

Mid Diagonal shroud (D2)

Batten

Fully battened mainsail

Floating backstay

Backstay

Lower diagonal shroud (D1)

Lower vertical shroud (V1)

Reef points

Compass

Staysail

Secondary winch

Topsail

Steering wheel

Pushpit or star

Starboard

Dodger

Primary winch

Halyard winch

Staysail sheet

Forehatch

Topsail sheet

Turnbuckle

Chainplates

Pulpit

Cleat

Roller furling drum

Chock

Port

FIGURE 2.3   The deck of a larger cruising boat, showing winches for the halyards, primary winches (used for the headsail sheets), and secondary winches (used for runners or spinnaker sheets). This boat has two headsails and is known as a cutter rig. It also has a keel that is not retractable into the hull. Notice that the gear is heavier, and that steering is done by a wheel rather than a tiller (as on the smaller boats).

which show the parts of three different styles of boats: a dinghy, a weekender, and a larger cruising sailboat.

Some dinghies, such as the Optimist shown in Figure 2.4, have only one sail, a mainsail, but most have a second sail called a jib that is set forward of the mainsail. These sails work most efficiently when the boat is sailing upwind—that is, into the wind at a slight angle. When the boat is sailing downwind (or in the same direction as the wind), a third sail, called a spinnaker, is often set. Other boats have two masts and set more than one sail on each mast. Figures 2.5 and 2.6 show the parts of different types of sails. Notice that the leading edge of a sail is always called the luff. On the spinnaker shown in Figure 2.7, for example, the luff is to the left, or port, side; if the boat gibes, the edge that is now the leach will become the luff.

Unfortunately, even many commonly used sailing terms are dying out as more people get into sailing. Rather than learning which side is port or starboard, many people prefer to say "left" or "right." But that's a whole 'nother story.

FIGURE 2.4 An Optimist dinghy from Vanguard Sailboats in Bristol, Rhode Island. Optimists are great boats for children learning to sail. *(photo courtesy of Vanguard Sailboats)*

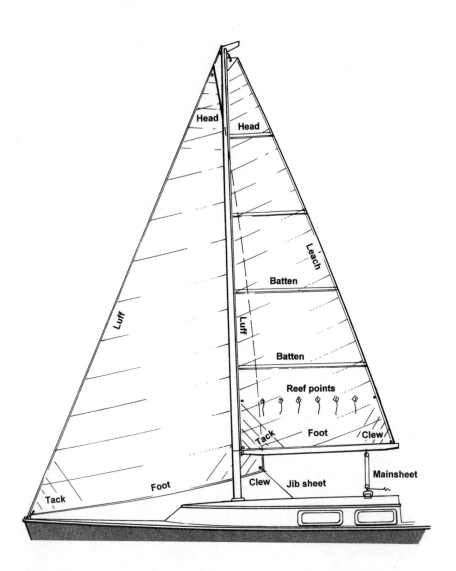

FIGURE 2.5   A typical sloop rig. Sheets are the ropes used to control the clew of the sail. Usually the mainsheet has a tackle on it so that the sail can be pulled in and eased quickly. Jib or genoa sheets do not have tackles on them.

HOISTING THE SAILS

As Captain Hooke said, "Step aboard, me 'earties." As you step aboard a boat for the first time, you may feel some of the same anx-

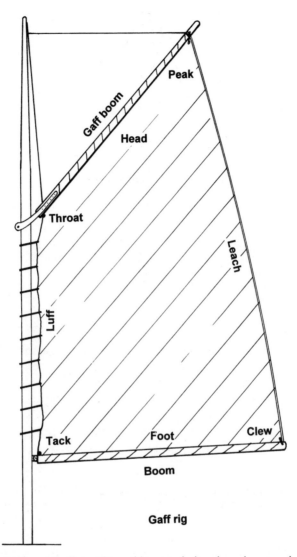

Gaff boom

Peak

Head

Throat

Leach

Luff

Tack

Foot

Clew

Boom

Gaff rig

FIGURE 2.6 A gaff rig. This sail has two halyards: a throat and a peak halyard. It's important to raise both halyards together to make it easy to raise the gaff.

iety as if Captain Hooke were your host. "What is going to happen now?" you wonder. Stop worrying, and just take things one step at a time.

The first thing to remember, if the boat is a dinghy, is not to stand on its edge. Standing on the edge of the boat, known as the

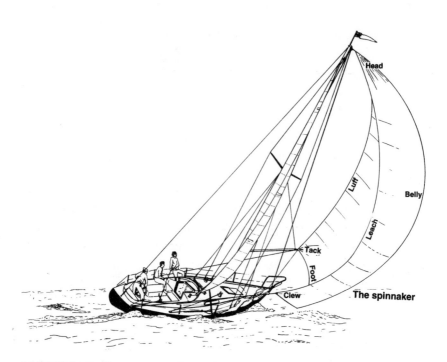

Labels on figure: Head, Belly, Luff, Leach, Tack, Foot, Clew, The spinnaker

FIGURE 2.7 A spinnaker under sail. Notice that the parts of this sail are the same as for other sails. When the boat gibes, the leach will become the luff and the spinnaker pole will be set on the other side

gunwale (pronounced *gunnel*), can tip the boat over and put everyone, including you, in the water. Try to step gently into the middle of the boat.

Once aboard the boat you sit in the cockpit amid a tangle of lines and sails. What comes next? First, find the mainsheet—that is, the rope that holds the mainsail—and untie it. It will need to be loose when you hoist the mainsail. Find the jib sheet and untie this rope as well. With both sheets untied, find the main halyard—the rope that hoists the mainsail. Look aloft and check that the main halyard is not tangled around the spreader (the horizontal piece of wood or aluminum that holds the shroud wires out from the mast) or another halyard. Make it a rule to check aloft before you connect any halyard to a sail. If the halyard is clean (not tangled), shackle it to the top of the mainsail. Now you are ready to hoist the mainsail. You may have to feed the top of the sail into a luff groove (which can be found on the back of the mast), or the mainsail may be attached with slides. Once the sail is ready, hoist away.

Support the boom as the sail lifts it off the deck; this reduces the strain on the leach (trailing edge) of the mainsail as it's hoisted. Pull the sail to the masthead and cleat, or tie off, the halyard in the appropriate place. The wind is probably causing the boom to bounce around a little. That's okay. Don't pull the sail in with the mainsheet or the boat will start to sail while you are still tied to the dock.

If you are alone, it is probably best not to set the jib now, but just to sail under mainsail. If you are with a crew, you should hoist the jib next. Make sure it's ready to be hoisted and that the halyard is clear aloft. Hoist the jib and cleat the halyard. Now you have two sails flapping.

Here comes the tricky part. Undo the dock lines and push off. Pull in on the mainsheet until the sail starts to drive the boat forward. Remember to watch out for other boats, hold the helm, and pull the mainsheet in. Someone will have to watch out for rocks, check the telltales on the mainsail, make sure there are no lines trailing in the water, get the fenders inboard, check the jib, and tell your crew where you want them to sit. It will all seem confusing until you get clear of the dock and settle down to steer the boat.

When you first start steering, you'll find that it's not like driving a car. If you push the tiller to one side, the boat keeps going around in a circle until you pull the tiller back to the centerline of the boat. When you first start, you'll wiggle and wobble all over the water. That's normal. Everyone started the same way. Sailors call it writing your name on the ocean, and even some very experienced sailors do it. It takes practice to keep the tiller centered. Gradually, you'll learn to move the tiller as little as possible. If you persevere, eventually you'll get a feel for the boat that transcends mere helming (*helming* is the word used for steering with a tiller or a wheel). You'll sense where the boat is going and correct it without even thinking.

Another job you may have to do while you are helming is trimming the mainsail. This is fairly easy as long as the sail is set up properly. Chapter 5 tells you how to set your sails up properly. Once again, you'll eventually be able to check the mainsail at a glance, and you'll sense whether it's too tight or too loose just by the feel of the boat. All these are things you'll learn when you get out on the water. While they may seem difficult now, they get easier with practice.

WHAT TO DO IF YOU CAPSIZE

Virtually the first thing every dinghy sailor learns is the capsizing drill: wearing your life jacket (as always) while you deliberately capsize your dinghy. Select a calm day and an area where the water is fairly shallow. This will prevent the boat from turning completely upside down, making it easier for you to get it back upright again.

Capsizing is quite easy on most dinghies. You stand on the edge of the boat and lean back. Over it goes! Now you have to get the boat back upright. If the centerboard is sticking out of the bottom of the boat, doing this is easy. Swim to the centerboard, reach up and hold on to the tip of the board, and pull downward. As the board comes down toward you, grasp the rail and pull the boat upright. A heavy boat might need the combined weight of you and your crew to haul it upright. If the centerboard isn't already down, you will have to pull it out of the centerboard slot before you can get the boat upright. If the board is stuck, you may be able to right the boat by pulling on the rail, but usually you need to use the leverage of the board.

Once the boat is upright, you should bail it out, put the lines back where they belong, and get sailing again. Because it's so easy to capsize a dinghy, you should always have a bailer and a sponge tied to the boat with a length of twine. Forget the twine and you may find that your bailer has floated away just when you need it.

If you find that you cannot get a capsized boat upright again, *do not swim away from the boat.* Stay with the boat. If possible, get out of the water and onto the upturned hull. If you stay in the water and it's cold, you will eventually get hypothermia. (For more on hypothermia, see Chapter 9.) Wave or shout to nearby boats and ask for help. It's easy for people to see an upturned boat with somebody standing on it. It's very hard to see a head in the water. (To get some idea of how hard it is to see a person swimming in the water, try dropping an old soccer ball or a basketball in the water as you sail along and note how long it takes you to lose sight of it. Unless you are watching very carefully, you will lose sight of it within a hundred yards.)

GOING AGROUND

Don't worry if you go aground. In most dinghies you simply pull the centerboard up and turn around to get away from the rocks or mud. It's when you are sailing very fast and go aground that you can do some damage. If the worst happens and you get stuck, in most dinghies you can simply hop over the side and push off. Beware a mud bottom, though. You could get stuck in the mud yourself!

HITTING ANOTHER BOAT

This is something you really want to avoid. Most boat owners get pretty irate when a dinghy sails into the side of their boat. It can cost several thousand dollars to repair severe scratches in the hull of a large boat, and you don't want to be liable for such a repair. Usually, if you are going to hit another boat—for example, you might not have enough speed to avoid drifting into the other craft—you can put a fender between the boats or push off the other boat to avoid colliding with it. But be careful: Getting a hand or finger caught between two boats is sure to make your eyes water!

These are a few of the basic things you need to know to get out on the water. As you read on, you'll learn more about handling a boat under sail, navigation, and some of the rules of the road. You don't have to know them to go sailing, but the more you know before you get out on the water, the more enjoyable your sailing will be.

CHAPTER 3

GETTING OUT ON THE WATER

Learning to sail is the first step toward an exciting new lifestyle. With your own boat you never have to find a hotel room; you don't even have to go to a marina. Your boat can become a home, a refuge, a workplace, a means of transportation, and an entertainment center all rolled into one. Given modern communications you don't even have to be within sight of land to talk to friends. Last year we sailed across the Atlantic Ocean, en route downloading data from the Internet while we were a thousand miles at sea. We sent e-mail messages to our families and talked regularly on the telephone. You *can* have it all on the modern sailing voyage.

More than 70 percent of the world is water, which means you can sail nearly three-quarters of it. When you are sailing, you'll see sights that you never knew existed. Once around 1 A.M., when we were sailing in the middle of the Atlantic, I saw two trails that looked just like torpedos from a World War II submarine heading straight for our boat. The trails passed under us as I headed for the bow and looked below the boat. Dolphins, their bodies illuminated with glowing trails of phosphorescence, gamboled all around us. For an hour this awesome display continued. We counted fourteen bottle-nosed dolphins, but there may have been more. Then as suddenly as they arrived, they left, and we went back to sailing alone in the dark ocean.

Another night we saw a huge flash light up the sky as bright as day. We heard a boat located more than a hundred miles away call the Coast Guard and report the flash. The Coast Guard, nearly eight hundred miles astern, had seen nothing. Was it a meteorite? An airplane? A missile test? We may never know, but it spanned over a hundred miles. We guessed it was a meteor that hit the earth's atmosphere and exploded. Would we have noticed it if we'd been ashore? I doubt it, with all the other stimuli to distract us.

SOME SAILING OPTIONS

When I learned to sail, I started in a dinghy. I remember the first time I sailed alone—the sense of freedom it gave me. I was hooked. From dinghies I graduated to sailing larger boats. Some of these boats we raced; others we cruised. Then came the first night of off-shore racing and a four-day cruise from La Rochelle, France, to Southampton, England. Gradually my skills increased.

After forty years of sailing I still learn something virtually every time I go out. You can learn, too, just by watching and asking questions. As your skills increase, you will graduate from sailing dinghies to sailing weekenders, overnight cruises, and maybe offshore races. All you need to do is learn as much as possible every time you go out on the water. And start to save for your dream sailboat.

Dinghy Sailing

If you decide to begin sailing in a dinghy, what type of craft should you look for? First, check at your local yacht club or sailing school, which probably has its own fleet of dinghies. For example, our local club has a fleet of Optimists and one of 420s. The Optimists are used to teach children to sail, while the 420s are for more advanced racers. By purchasing a dinghy like these at your own yacht club, you are assured that somebody close by knows how to sail and maintain it, and also that you may be able to race it. Plus you will probably have a place to launch your boat and, if you become a member, a place to socialize after the sailing.

(You could also look at Olympic-class dinghies if you have any aspirations in this direction. These classes tend to change every four years or so. But before you travel this road, make sure you have the time and commitment.)

Dinghies have a huge advantage over most boats in that they can be used for exploring very shallow creeks as well as sailing in deeper waters. You can sail one on dammed waters, lakes, or ocean fringes, then float it onto a trailer and rig it in a few minutes. All you need is a place to launch the boat. (Obviously, you should figure a trailer in with the cost of the dinghy.)

Weekending

The next step up from dinghy sailing is a small sailboat for sailing on weekends and camping out in different harbors. Usually the best size is between twenty and twenty-six feet. (See Figure 3.1.) Unlike a dinghy, the weekender may have a small stove, an ice chest (which may be a portable), and storage space for dry foods. It will probably have an outboard engine with a gas tank in the cockpit. Also unlike the dinghy, the weekender will have real bunks. There may only be a vee berth on the forepeak and a pair of quarter berths aft, but it will still be a far cry from sleeping under a boom tent on a cold, windy night.

Weekenders tend to be light and, like a dinghy, they may capsize, but don't let this put you off. They can be launched off a trailer or kept in the water in a marina or on a mooring. Having a boat that can be launched off a trailer opens up many new waters to sail. For example, a friend has a trailer-sailer, as they are sometimes called, and he launches his boat off the trailer. Normally he sails at his home lake, but he'll travel to new lakes and man-made reservoirs when he wants to explore. This way he gets to sail in some of the finest waters in the country. For a long vacation he might trail the boat to one of the Great Lakes and sail for a week or two. He also fishes from his sailboat and has a great time. Because he can tow his boat to any destination he likes, he has made a lot of new friends all over the country.

Singlehanding

Later, when the sailing bug has really bitten, you might find you can't get crew to go with you every time you sail. No problem; you can singlehand your boat. Singlehanding is a little more arduous

FIGURE 3.1   For weekending and small-boat fun, the Ultimate 20 is the ultimate one-design speedster. *(photo by Patrick Short, courtesy of Ultimate Sailboats)*

than sailing with a crew, but it can be very enjoyable. I remember one trip when I was delivering a boat. The wind was out of the north on a bright, sunny day, and I set my largest spinnaker for the fifty-mile sail. The trip took most of the day, but what did I care? I was thoroughly enjoying myself.

Singlehanding requires that you prepare carefully, mentally rehearsing every move before you make it. I would not have set a spinnaker if the weather had looked as if it might blow. To set the spinnaker, I went through each step carefully, making sure each line was fastened before I proceeded with the next step. To take the spinnaker down required even more preparation, because this boat was not set up for singlehanding.

Every operation on a singlehanded boat requires forethought and preparation. If you do not prepare, you will end up having problems. Preparation means that you think through every maneuver and then lay out the required lines, sails, or other gear before you attempt to do anything.

When you begin to execute a maneuver, do it as quickly as possible to ensure that no problems develop. Then clean up immediately. If you are singlehanding for the first time, don't try anything too ambitious. Simply set the sails and go from A to B. You will find that leaving the dock and coming alongside are often the hardest jobs.

When you are leaving the dock, put the dock lines onboard, make sure they are not trailing in the water, and motor clear of the harbor. When you are clear and have room to let go of the helm, clean up the dock lines and fenders. Hoist sail by letting the boat power slowly into the wind under the autopilot, or simply put the brake on the helm and let the boat drift. Get the mainsail up first and make any helm corrections; then get the jib up. Clean up and sheet in. Now turn off the engine. While you are hoisting sail, keep the engine ready to correct your course or help you avoid buoys or other boats.

When you come back into a harbor, simply stop at the entrance; if the wind is blowing too strongly for this, find a suitable lee before dropping sails and motoring to your slip. Bring the boat into the slip and stop it dead alongside before attempting to step off and tie up dock lines. If you are having difficulty getting alongside, call the marina on the VHF and have somebody meet you at your slip. Remember also to wear a harness or life jacket at all times when you are singlehanding. Frankly, I prefer a harness so I won't fall overboard, especially if the water is cold (in the spring, for instance).

Many boats can be singlehanded. But if you are going to singlehand on a regular basis, you should fit your boat with roller-furling headsails and other gear that make it easier to handle alone. Also invest in an autopilot and GPS (Global Positioning System), so the boat can continue on course while you are making coffee or tidying up the deck. Many singlehanders install an electronic radar detector that tells them from which direction a large ship might be approaching. And they keep an almost constant lookout to make sure they are not surprised by another boat bearing down on them. Only when you have a lot of experience should you sleep while singlehanding.

Singlehanding can easily become an enjoyable way of life, but you do need to be aware of your limits, and you need to prepare carefully. If you singlehand at any time, be sure that somebody on shore knows your destination and estimated time of arrival. This way, if you do get into trouble, somebody can be alerted to find the boat and, I hope, you.

Multihulls

If you are looking for the exhilaration of maximum speed in sailing, a multihull is the way to go. Multihulls have been sailed around the world, recording some amazing noon-to-noon runs. (The runs are measured from noon to noon because a ship's location used to be found by shooting the sun with a sextant at noon.) Not only do they sail faster than monohulls, but they also have more accommodations and heel less. Although multihulls can turn over if you don't watch the heel angle carefully, capsizes are not that common.

There are two major types of multihulls, catamarans and trimarans, although proas and outriggers can be considered multihulls, too. Catamarans have two hulls, like the one shown in Figure 3.2, usually equipped with accommodations in each. Quite often, especially in the larger cats, there is an accommodation in the bridge deck as well. This gives a forty-foot catamaran more than double the space of a comparable monohull. Catamarans do not heel like monohulls, although they may raise one hull out of the water occasionally. Normally, their heel angle is less than fifteen degrees.

Catamarans get their stability by spacing the hulls some distance apart. Without the enormous lump of lead that monohulls use to keep them upright, catamarans often sail at speeds double those of a similar monohull. With twice the accommodations and twice the speed for the same sail area, it's a wonder to me that you don't see more of them on the water. If you want to try sailing a

FIGURE 3.2   You don't have to sail a monohull. This multihulled C420 catamaran is available from Vanguard Sailboats. *(photo courtesy of Vanguard Sailboats)*

catamaran before buying one, you can charter a craft from the Catamaran Company in Ft. Lauderdale, Florida, which specializes in catamaran charters. The firm sails them in the Caribbean during the winter and points farther north during the summer.

Like catamarans, trimarans are fast, but they may have less space. The fastest tris have accommodations in the central hull, with outriggers (also called amas) on either side. These usually provide a large part of the buoyancy of the boat, so that if they get submerged, the boat won't trip over them and capsize.

CRUISING CHOICES

Cruising is one of the most delightful aspects of sailing. It's estimated that more than 90 percent of sailors are cruisers, sailing from one place to another for the sheer joy of being out on the water. Cruising has many faces—from gunkholing to coastal cruising and cruising across seas and oceans.

Gunkholing

Gunkholing is a sailor's term for exploring narrow rivers, estuaries, and streams. It's usually done by folks who want to venture off the beaten track in smaller boats. Generally, gunkholers are centerboard or shallow-draft boats that allow sailors to step into very shallow water or onto dry land. Gunkholing can be fun if you want to explore a limited-access natural area such as a salt marsh, but boats intended for gunkholing should generally not be used out in the ocean.

Coastal Cruising

Of all the types of cruising available, coastal cruising is probably the most common. Whether you sail from marina to marina or wander from your home port to secluded coves, coastal cruising is fun. The time you spend sailing is limited only by your imagination. You can set up a destination that is one hour, or ten hours, or even days away. You set the pace and the goals.

Preparing for a coastal cruise should be done carefully. Make sure you have all the Coast Guard–required items onboard before you start, and include enough food for the duration of the trip plus one-third more, just in case you get stuck or lost. You should also plan to carry charts of all your destinations, along with one or two additional charts for harbors to duck into along the way should the weather turn bad. In case fog comes in, you should have a foghorn. (If it's an aerosol type, have a couple of extra cans of air.) And just in case you get caught out at night, make sure you have flashlights and extra batteries onboard. Carry a first-aid kit, too, and have some training in its use. You can call for emergency medical help with your VHF radio should anything go seriously wrong.

Before you go cruising, check the forecast and make sure your weather window does not include any potential storms. Cruising in a major storm with a rocky coast a few miles to leeward is not recommended. If the forecast is for bad weather, don't push it, even if you are headed for home and feel you must arrive on time. Call your boss to say that you are stuck, or leave your boat and go home by car or train. You can always bring your boat home when the weather is more suitable. With today's long-range weather forecasts, there is no reason why a coastal cruiser should get caught out in a storm.

Ocean Cruising

Although ocean cruising can provide enormous pleasure, novice sailors will likely be guests and not crew members on such a trip. Preparation for going offshore takes a great deal of time and involves every part of the boat and of the crew members' lives. Entire books have been written about sailing offshore; this is merely a brief introduction. The first step is for the captain to set a date—not a hard-and-fast date, but a soft one that can be modified if the weather turns bad or the boat isn't ready.

The next step is to plan your route by estimating the speed at which your boat can sail and approximately how far you can go in a day. Just as in coastal cruising, you will obtain charts for each part of the route. Similarly, if your journey takes you along coasts, you should have extra charts for a few harbors that you may need to duck into in bad weather. You'll also need an offshore chart on which to mark your route. This type of chart, posted where the entire crew can see it, serves as a good record of your progress. (See Figure 3.3.) At this stage you cannot plan your trip in infinite detail, but you can make a skeleton outline that will indicate where you expect to be at any time.

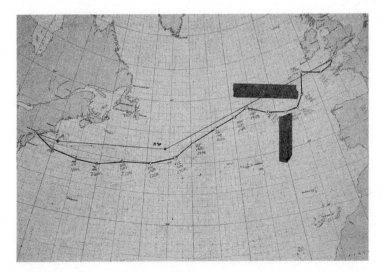

FIGURE 3.3   A chart of a trans-Atlantic crossing. The estimated route is shown above the actual route. The black marks are pieces of tape used to mark the location of a dolphin sighting.

The biggest job before you leave is to perform a thorough inspection of your boat. If you are in doubt about any part, replace it. Sod's law says that whatever breaks is something you noticed was wearing out but didn't bother to repair or replace—and it's almost always something for which you do not have spares. Carry a notebook when inspecting your boat and write everything down. Sod's law also says that everything you forget to write down will haunt you when you are at sea.

After every item has been checked, get a spares kit for all the mechanical items. (If you get the spares kit before you make your checks, you'll use most of the spares making repairs.) In addition, you should have a good set of tools. At the very least carry wire cutters (if your rigging is wire) or a hacksaw and plenty of spare blades for rod rigging.

While you are preparing and storing, don't forget a good first-aid kit. (See page 130.) These are available from many sources and should include a supply of any prescription drugs you are taking. Also include plenty of sunblock and sunburn cream.

Food is another big concern for ocean cruising. For long trips you have two options: One is to freeze as much as you can and use fresh foods first, then frozen goods, and finally canned foods; the other is to stock freeze-dried foods and plenty of water. Freeze-dried foods can also be stored for emergency use as long as you have enough water to reconstitute them.

As a backup, carry several additional packets of freeze-dried and canned goods. This way, if you run into light winds and the trip takes longer than expected, you will still be able to feed the crew. I normally plan on having at least 30 to 35 percent more food than I'll need.

RACING

Racing sailboats is, in my opinion, one of the most pressure-filled, exciting, and interesting of sports. Being in a fleet of a hundred or more boats and winning the race is as exhilarating as any victory you can imagine—especially if you know that your skills made the difference.

Novice sailors who go racing will learn more about handling their boat, handling other people, and organizing to win than they could in virtually any other situation. You'll learn when and how to change sails without losing very much speed, when to use a tidal stream to your advantage, and how to make your boat go in very light winds when cruising sailors are turning on their engines.

Unlike cruising, racing means you go out when the race starts, regardless of whether the weather is going to turn bad. Thus you'll probably face more storms and bad weather than the average cruising sailor. Consequently, you will learn how to sail harder and how to push your boat in weather heavier than most cruising sailors ever see.

During one Fastnet race we set a spinnaker when it was blowing nearly thirty knots. The spinnaker lasted for about six hours before it blew out; we set twin headsails poled out. We finished second in this race. The boat that won flew a spinnaker for more than ten hours. If we hadn't learned how to carry sail in very heavy winds, we wouldn't have placed. The thrill of surging down the back of waves and watching the knotmeter climb to twelve or fourteen knots cannot be described. Figure 3.4 shows our boat returning from the Fastnet Rock in leftover gale-force seas.

How do you get started in racing sailboats? There are several ways. The easiest is to participate in your local yacht-club events and gradually build a reputation as a good sailor. Quite often you'll be asked to sail with an owner who needs crew. Another way is to post a notice on the yacht club's bulletin board. You might not get on the fastest boats to start with, but you can work your way up to them. Yet another method is to call an owner and ask for a berth. Quite often an owner may not have enough crew for a particular race. When you get aboard the boat, work as hard as possible to help the boat win. Volunteer to pack the spinnaker, or to make the coffee. Do what you need to do to get noticed, be willing to accept any assignment within your experience—and you may get asked back.

Dinghy Racing

If you want to start racing, begin with dinghy racing. A small boat will give you a greater appreciation of the vagaries of the wind. You see and react almost immediately to a slight wind shift, whether it's a header or a lift. (If it *is* a header, the conventional wisdom is to

FIGURE 3.4 Boat returning from the Fastnet Rock in leftover gale-force seas.

stand into it and then tack.) You'll also see how other boats are sailing and where they are going to pick up extra wind. Quite often dinghy racing crews are chosen during the winter meetings at the yacht club, when the helmsman (often the dinghy owner) starts looking for a crew for the next season. If you learn of a helmsman without a crew, volunteer to sail with him or her. It may lead to a more permanent arrangement. If you have crewed for a while and have your own boat, give a new crew a chance to learn the ropes, if your regular crew can't make it. You may find a gem in the rough.

You will probably lose your first few races. Don't lose heart. Typically, dinghies race as a class; every boat is the same. This makes it easy to learn by watching the winners. For example, when my son David took part in his first race, I told him to watch the sailors who had been sailing for a long time: "See how they rig their boat," I said, "how they set up and trim their sails, how they sit in the boat, and how they position themselves on the race course, and then try to figure out why they do what they do." David watched and learned. In his first race he was second to the most experienced sailor in the fleet. When I asked him how he'd done it, David said, "I watched him and followed him." He subsequently placed in several more races by watching what the leaders were doing. His younger brother, Michael, followed David's example and placed equally well.

Watching the leaders also involves talking to them after a race to find out why they made a particular maneuver or used a certain tactic. Gradually, you will learn how to get the best from the dinghy you are sailing. Some sailors never feel that they have learned everything there is to know about racing one type of dinghy; they continue to race the craft for many years. Others step up into larger boats and begin the process again.

Day Racing

Day racing is just what it's name implies—racing a sailboat during the daytime. At the end of each day the boats return to harbor, and the crews often have dinner or a party together. This is a great way to meet more sailors and generally have a lot of fun. The pinnacle of day racing, of course, is the America's Cup, which is a best-of-seven series. In this instance, the competition is fierce and the camaraderie much more intense.

Overnight Racing

Races longer than sixty or seventy miles tend to be overnight and are frequently referred to as offshore races. When I first sailed offshore racing boats, we'd start a race on Friday night and return sometime on Sunday. The courses were usually more than two hundred miles long, and raced every other weekend. When we didn't race offshore, we held day races on Saturday and Sunday. The schedule was hectic because we usually raced Tuesday and

Thursday evenings as well. Today you won't find so many overnight races; the trend has been to concentrate more on day racing.

Offshore or Ocean Racing

Offshore racing can trace its roots all the way back to the nineteenth century. In 1866 businessman Pierre Lorrillard challenged two other men to a race across the Atlantic Ocean. Each put up thirty thousand dollars, and their boats, the *Henrietta, Vespa,* and *Fleetwing,* set sail in December 1866. After 2,998 miles of racing—from Sandy Hook, New Jersey, to the Lizard near Falmouth, England—*Henrietta* won the prize money and *Fleetwing* lost six men overboard. In 1908 the first offshore race to Bermuda was held, and in 1925 the first Fastnet race was run.

Today, if we exclude round-the-world events, the big three offshore races are the 628-mile Fastnet, the 635-mile Bermuda, and the 620-mile Sidney-Hobart. Most of the other long races are around two hundred miles and can be comfortably completed in a weekend.

In recent years there has been a trend toward very long ocean races, such as the Whitbread Round-the-World race. From their early days—when an average cruising boat had a chance to win—these races have evolved into high-tech, high-pressure marathons. For example, the crew on a Whitbread 60 have barely enough room to stand up below deck. They live on freeze-dried foods moistened with water from a reverse-osmosis water maker and endure weeks of icy-cold sailing in very strong winds. To race under these conditions requires a high degree of compatibility on the part of the crew and support team. It also requires a large amount of money, which explains why virtually every boat is sponsored.

If the America's Cup is the Super Bowl of match racing, the Admiral's Cup is the World Series of offshore racing. The Admiral's Cup is contested by teams of three boats. Each team races for one country, and there have been as many as nineteen teams competing. The format has changed considerably since I first participated in this series; it now involves a race of around two hundred miles, two or three inshore races in Christchurch Bay, and the Fastnet race. A boat's position in each race accumulates points, and the team with the most points wins the cup.

THE AMERICA'S CUP The America's Cup is the pinnacle of match racing. The race originated in 1851 when the schooner *America* raced against a fleet of English yachts around the Isle of Wight in England. The prize, then known as the Hundred Guinea Cup, was brought back to America and given to the New York Yacht Club in 1857, when it was renamed the America's Cup. The deed of gift stipulated that it was to be a perpetual challenge cup and the property of the club that won it. And it could be challenged for by any club in the world. Since those early days the deed of gift has been modified somewhat, and after the court fight of 1987–88 it was amended so that a board of trustees, comprised of one member from each of the winning clubs, made decisions regarding the cup rather than a judicial court.

Only one club can be a challenger (the challenger of record). But part of being challenger of record is that all the challenging yachts compete in a series of races. The winner of the challenger series becomes the challenger regardless of whether the boat belongs to the same club as the challenger of record. The defender holds a separate series to determine the winner and the defender and challenger meet in the final.

The cost of an America's Cup campaign can be very high. Typically, twenty-eight to thirty-five million dollars is required over three to five years to participate.

CHARTERING

There are many styles and types of boats and many facets to sailing. Once you have learned to sail, you can try any of them by chartering. This involves renting a boat for a set period of time ranging from a few hours to an afternoon, a day, a week, or several weeks.

When you charter, you rent the craft either bareboat (uncrewed) or as a crewed charter.

Bareboat Chartering

When you bareboat charter, the charterer usually requires some proof that you know how to sail. Once you've reached this stage, you can set sail to wherever you want to go. Most large charter companies have boats from thirty to sixty feet available in various ports of the world. The Caribbean islands, Florida, and other warm areas are best in the winter months, while northern ports have boats available during summer. You can find charter companies listed in the back of many sailing magazines (try *Soundings* or *Sail*), or you can check your yellow pages for a local charterer.

The most common restrictions in chartering are that you be back on time and that you do not damage the boat. Sometimes restrictions are also placed on the area in which you can sail, or the number of people you can take aboard. You are responsible for providing the food, drinks, and any visas required, as well as for the well-being of your crew. Typically, the charterer may offer to provision your boat at an extra cost. Many bareboat charter sailors provision only lightly, eating ashore most evenings. The cost of chartering bareboat varies according to the area, the time of year, and the size of the boat. Often charter companies run fleets of boats for bareboat charters. You can call and get information from virtually any charter company.

Crewed Charters

When you charter a crewed boat, generally through a broker, you will usually find that the boat has a captain, a crew, and/or a cook onboard. Going on a crewed charter is often like staying in a moving luxury hotel. Step aboard, and the crew takes you wherever you want to go. You may or may not be permitted to help out with the sailing. Usually, all meals will be served at the times you wish, and often you will be served exactly what you like (depending on its availability in the local market).

Chartering a crewed boat is more expensive than a bareboat charter, plus you are expected to tip the crew when the charter is over. Typically, these tips range from a hundred dollars per person per night to 10 to 15 percent of the charter fee. If you want to find a charter broker, you can check with most yacht brokers, who are often connected with a charter broker. You can also look in sailing magazines. Charter brokers can book charters all over the world. The good ones will tell you what to expect, right down to the weather and what clothes to take along.

Your sailing experience will be what you make it. It all starts with that first step—going to a sailing school or going out with friends and getting hooked. The sport can become an all-consuming passion or it can simply be another pleasant form of recreation. You get to choose how and where you do it. That is the beauty of sailing.

CHAPTER 4

BASIC BOAT-HANDLING TECHNIQUES

You have learned about the wind, the water, and the parts of the boat, and now you are going to set sail on your own for the first time. It feels great to be in command, but you are also nervous. You don't want to put the boat aground, bang into another boat, or get anyone hurt.

Once you're on the water you sense of enjoyment and freedom will be wonderful—even though you are also bound to make mistakes. I remember once backing down a boat to turn it around and promptly wrapping a mooring buoy around the prop. Embarrassing, yes, but not half as embarrassing as getting naked in the middle of the harbor and diving under the boat to cut away the mooring line.

In the following section I'll go through the sequence as if you are setting out on a boat. This should give you an idea of the order in which things happen.

PICKING A DAY

Begin your sailing adventure by putting to sea in light winds. After all, you wouldn't go down an expert ski slope on your first trip down a mountain. Light winds give you time to react and let you remember simple things—such as lowering the centerboard.

GETTING ABOARD

I once watched a small dinghy with five people onboard heading out to a sailboat on a mooring. As the dinghy neared the yacht, the helmsman slowed the outboard and allowed the dinghy to drift toward the sailboat. When it was in range, everyone aboard the dinghy stood up and reached for the boat rail. The weight of the entire crew moving proved to be too much for the dinghy, which promptly capsized. The splash was awesome! Even funnier was the sight of the dinghy crew draped like dirty laundry along the side of the boat, holding on by their fingertips.

This, of course, is not the way to board a boat on a mooring. If you have to step out of a dinghy onto a boat, stay seated until you are safely alongside; only then should you climb aboard. And when stepping onto a boat from a dinghy, remember my earlier advice: Try not to stand on the gunwale or you will probably capsize.

To make matters even easier, bring the boat alongside a dock so you can simply step aboard. Of course, even this method has its perils. Make sure that the boat is tied securely to the dock, and that you can step across the gap. I once tried to step across a gap as the crew, not hearing my shout over the roar of the engine, looked to seaward and left the dock. The splash certainly got a lot of laughs!

Your first time steering a boat will probably be, as a well-known advertisement says, "an adventure in moving." The boat is moving, you are moving trying to control all the equipment, and your mind is moving (at ultra-high speed) as you try to figure out what is happening. But after a few days on the water you'll start to feel more confident. Here's how to begin.

GETTING UNDER WAY

Now that you are aboard and dry, it's time to get under sail. The techniques you'll use will depend on whether you're leaving the dock or a mooring. In either case, though, you'll have to hoist your sails.

Watch the Wind Direction

Another trick that you'll learn very early is to start sailing when the wind is blowing parallel to the dock or beach, or slightly toward it. Watching a beginner sail away from the beach or dock when the wind is blowing directly onto it can be hilarious for onlookers, but not so funny for the person in the boat. To sail away from the beach in these conditions, you have to sail upwind. This means you should have the centerboard down. Of course, if you are close to the beach you won't be able to drop the board, so you'll try sailing without it. The boat will go sideways and you'll end up on the beach again, or you'll try to put the board down too soon and plunge it into the mud, stopping the boat dead. If you try to sail away from a dock under the same conditions, chances are the wind will blow you back onto it before you have time to get up some speed.

If the wind is blowing away from the dock or beach, you'll be able to sail away easily enough, but you might have to ask for a tow to get back if you haven't mastered sailing upwind yet. This might be embarrassing, but don't worry. Virtually all sailors have made a fool of themselves at one time or another. What if there are no other boats around to tow you? The sea may not be very forgiving, and you may be in serious trouble. For this reason, try to have a friend around in a chase boat should you get into trouble.

If in Doubt, Let It Out

Imagine your first experience stepping into a sailboat. You look at the mess of lines, folded sails, and all manner of cleats, blocks, and tracks. How will you ever figure out what goes where? Plus you have to learn about the weather, where the wind comes from, how much the boat should heel, and where the rocks are. It seems overwhelming, even a little frightening. Don't worry; you'll learn. If anything goes wrong and it looks like the boat is getting into trouble, just remember a simple rule: "If in doubt, let it out." On a small boat this means you should let go of everything: the tiller and the lines holding the sails. If none of the lines are cleated, the sails will flap, the boat will come upright, and you can figure out the problem before pulling the sails in and getting under way again.

WHAT'S IN A NAME? The term *starboard* is reputed to come from the times of Viking ships, when the steerboard (or steering board) was always placed on the right side of the vessel. In the days of wooden ships and iron men, *larboard* was the term used for the opposite side of the vessel. But imagine being at the top of a mast in a high wind and hearing a shout: "Grab the . . . arbord line and haul!" Did he say *larboard* or *starboard*? You don't have time to ask for clarification; you have to get the line in before the sail is flogged to pieces. For this reason, *port* became the term of choice for the left-hand side of the boat when facing the bow. Some say the term was chosen because port is the side on which boats were moored—to keep the steer-board away from the dock and potential damage. An easy way to remember which side is port (when facing the bow) is that the word *port* has four letters, and so does the word *left*. Port wine is red, and so is a port light.

HELMING

My entire family went sailing one day with a friend who owned a fifty-five-footer. My son Michael, who was eight years old at the time, was offered a chance to helm the vessel. It was the very first time he'd laid his hands on the helm of a big boat; he had to stand on the seat to see forward. After he had steered for a few minutes, his ear-to-ear grin said that he would be a sailor for life. Indeed, the thrill of steering a big boat for the first time is something he and every other sailor will remember for their entire lives. It is a feeling of being in control, of knowing where you are going, and of being free of the constraints imposed by being on land.

Helming is just another name for controlling a boat's rudder, and ultimately its direction. On a dinghy you use a tiller to control the rudder. On a larger boat you'll use a wheel, just like a car. In both cases, there are a few simple rules that, if followed, will let you helm the boat properly. First, remember that there are no lines marking which lane to sail in. (The exception is in some traffic-control areas near harbor entrances; even then, the lines are not painted on the surface of the sea.) So how do you go in a straight line? The answer is to determine the direction you want to go in and then find an object to sail toward. This object can be a buoy or some visible object on shore, such as a house—anything stationary can serve as a mark. All you need to do now is watch the mark and sail toward it. Sounds simple, doesn't it? And it *is* simple, until you go out of sight of land.

TRAFFIC SEPARATION SCHEMES Many of the harbors that see lots of vessels going in and out have a traffic separation zone. Inbound traffic usually keeps to one side, outbound traffic to other (see Chapter 8). These traffic "lanes" are intended to prevent ships from colliding in fog or reduced visibility. To find out if your harbor has a traffic separation scheme, you need to check a chart of the area (charts are maps of the sea). This usually shows the traffic lanes in a different shade or color from the surrounding area, with arrows indicating the direction of travel. When you go sailing, you should adhere to these traffic lanes as much as you can, and if you have to cross them, do it as fast as possible without cutting across the bow of an oncoming ship.

This is when you should remember the words of poet John Masefield and find a star to steer by. Unfortunately, you can only see stars at night, so when you sail out of sight of land, use your compass to set the boat on course and then look for a cloud or star in front of you, or note the angle of the sun relative to you. Sail the boat keeping the bow under the cloud, or to the sun's angle, and check the compass regularly because the cloud will move.

You should never stare at the compass and follow it. If you do, you'll steer a wavy course all over the ocean. During one night race I was off watch and was woken up by a thunderous crash. I dashed on deck, expecting to see the rig fallen over the side. But that hadn't happened. The boom crashing across the boat had woken me.

The person on the helm had fallen into the trap of steering by the compass, and had gradually increased the oscillations until the boat had gibed uncontrollably. The compass moves only after the bow of the boat has moved, so if the boat has already turned off course, the compass moves, and the helmsman turns the wheel to correct the turn. As the compass moves back to its original position the helmsman tries to correct the course, but the bow keeps on swinging. Gradually the oscillations build until control is lost.

The ideal is to correct an off-course movement before the boat gets too far off course. This means that you need to watch the bow relative to a mark ahead of the boat, and to correct the turn before the bow swings past its original position. This way you'll steer a much straighter course.

Good helmsmen pride themselves on steering a straight course. To do so takes skill, which takes time to learn. The best way to learn is to make small movements of the helm. Let the bow move around a little, but keep the helm movement as small as possible.

After you have learned to steer in a straight line, you need to learn how to turn the boat. "That's easy," you might say; "I just spin the wheel." True, you just spin the wheel, but when I worked with an America's Cup team I found that one helmsman consistently came out of a tack higher and faster than another one. The faster helmsman had learned how to tack the boat expertly, while the slower one hadn't.

In order to tack the boat you need to understand some theory. A rudder is much like an airplane wing. Air flowing past this wing creates lift; if the plane is put into a steep climb, the wings might stall, lift might disappear, and the plane might crash. In the boat's case, the keel and rudder create lift. Although a boat is unlikely to crash in this situation, a stall may occur when the rudder is put hard over. In other words, turning the rudder hard over may stall the rudder blade and reduce its ability to turn the boat.

In order to turn the boat properly, you should put the rudder over gently. Then, as the boat turns, you can increase the rudder angle. Before the boat reaches its new course, begin to straighten up the helm. If you bang the helm across, it's highly likely that the boat will sag off below the new course; you will have to bring it up to the course and wait for speed to build up. If you put the helm across too slowly, you will find that the boat virtually stops before the sails fill on the other tack, and you will have to sag off to leeward to build speed again. Tacking, then, requires a compromise between turning too slowly to the right angle and putting the helm over too hard, stalling the rudder. (See Figure 4.1.)

Turning through a gibe is even more difficult. In a gibe the boom will come crashing across the boat if the helm is put over too hard. Ideally, you gradually bring the boat to a sailing angle where the wind is blowing directly down its centerline from astern. Steer on this course long enough for the crew to pull in the mainsheet (this pulls in the mainsail), then let it out on the other side of the boat. If this is done properly, the mainsail will not bang across the boat, and you'll have time to warn everybody to keep their heads down. (At this point the jib is still on the original side.) Only after the mainsail is across should you turn the boat onto the other gibe. Then the jib is brought across and sheeted in. (See Figure 4.2.)

CREWING

The sign on the yacht-club notice board is innocuous enough. CREW WANTED FOR TUESDAY NIGHT RACING, it says. CALL FRED. So you

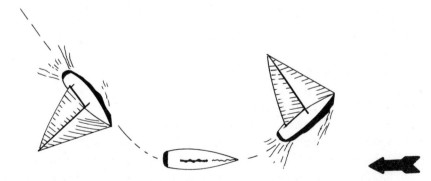

FIGURE 4.1   A boat tacks by turning the bow through the wind.

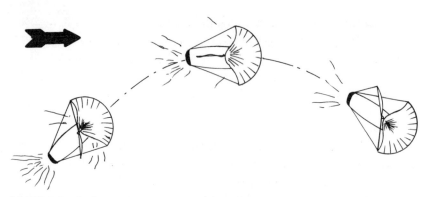

FIGURE 4.2   The stern passes through the wind when a boat gibes.

call Fred. He seems a nice guy, very pleasant at the yacht-club bar, and easygoing. You decide that you'll volunteer to crew in his dinghy. That first Tuesday you go out on Fred's boat. Sailing out to the start is fun; the two of you talk, and Fred tells you what he wants you to do. You nod and remember half of it. Then the ten-minute gun goes off and so does Fred.

"Get the jib in!" "Ease it out!" "Get your weight out!" "Watch out for that boat!" "Get the jib in!" "Get the board down!" Fred has turned into a raging tyrant. Some "Freds" shout and scream in the hope that you'll do things faster; unfortunately, this usually causes confusion and slows the entire process. I know of one dinghy sailor who simply stepped off the boat when Fred started screaming at him. He swam over to the committee boat and escaped.

Crewing aboard somebody else's boat is great if the helmsman and the crew talk to each other and work together. That's the whole idea of crewing: to work together to sail the boat as well as possible. To be a good crew, you need to know what the helmsman intends to do, which takes practice. Before racing you should practice with the helmsman to make sure you both know what is required. This is when you'll learn how to work together—and also whether the helmsman will turn into a star or a screamer.

As a crew you also need to be able to read the wind, trim the sails, set the right sail when required, and balance the boat with your weight if the helmsman needs it. On larger boats there will usually be more crew, each with a specific job, but their work still hinges on what the helmsman does or wants to do.

One of the crew's jobs is to be an extra pair of eyes for the helmsman. You have to be able to tell the helmsman when a puff of wind is coming. Do this by watching the wind shadow move across the water upwind of the boat. Small ripples that cause a slightly darker patch of water show a puff moving across the water. Quite often the puff will be a header—that is, the wind moves slightly ahead, making it necessary for the helmsman to bear off a little and sail slightly farther away from the wind. If the puff is strong, the boat will heel more and tend to turn into the wind. If the helmsman is ready, he can counter the boat's turn into the wind and use the puff to increase boat speed.

Another of the crew's jobs is to keep the jib trimmed perfectly at all times. This isn't difficult if the jib has telltales; simply adjust the sails until all the telltales flow aft perfectly. (See the section on sail trim, pages 64–70.)

It's when the crew has to keep the headsail full and also set the spinnaker that the going gets a little scarier. I recall my first memorable attempt at setting a spinnaker. We were rounding a mark and I had everything ready—except that the spinnaker had other ideas. It blew out of the bag, under the boat, and we stopped dead. Seconds later I managed to capsize the boat as I leaned over to leeward to try to retrieve it. I was not the most popular crew at that particular moment.

The lesson I learned from this encounter was to make sure that the spinnaker stays in the bag when it's about to be set. Over the years I have learned that there are many such lessons. One of them is to make sure all the lines are clipped to the right corners. A spinnaker has three corners, and unless each one is clearly marked it's very easy to clip the halyard to the wrong one.

I once sailed with the English prime minister Sir Edward Heath, and we had one of the best crews in England. During one race we hoisted the spinnaker as we rounded the weather mark. It was a very clean set; we didn't realize that we had screwed up until the head of the spinnaker reached the block at the corner of the transom. Unfortunately, it seemed like every photographer in England was watching at that moment, and we made news with our classic screwup. Setting a spinnaker improperly is very easy, which is why the crew needs to check everything at least twice.

In addition to setting and taking down the spinnaker, you'll be asked to judge the boat's position on the starting line. Before the start the boat should be sailed down this line; at this time you should check the alignment of shoreside marks. By knowing how marks line up on shore, you can easily tell how close or far away from the starting line the boat is. As the boat approaches the line, check the marks and talk the helmsman up or down so the boat starts the race right on the line.

Crewing, then, is a great opportunity. It allows you to sail on boats that you might never get aboard in any other way. It requires a lot of hard work, a commitment of large blocks of time, and a dedication to be the best that only comes with practice.

CHAPTER 5

BOAT HANDLING II: THE ADVENTURE CONTINUES

The hardest part of going sailing is leaving and returning to the dock. Getting safely out of a slip can be tricky, as can leaving a mooring buoy without running it over. When you return to the dock, whether under sail or under power, you don't want to come alongside with a crash. A nice gentle landing tells the world you know what you are doing. So learn the sequences for getting ready to sail, going sailing, and coming back into harbor without crashes and splashes.

SOME BASIC SAILING TECHNIQUES

Once you have learned that capsizing is relatively easy to handle, the next step is to learn how to manipulate the sails, helm the boat, watch the wind, watch for other boats, and keep your boat upright. It sounds like a lot of work, but if you take it one step at a time, you can easily manage every facet of sailing. In this section you'll be introduced to a few basic but essential sailing techniques.

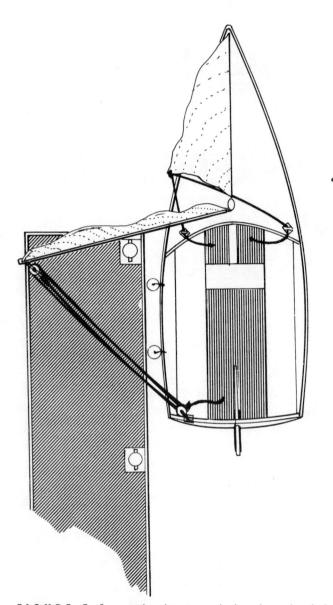

Wind direction

FIGURE 5.1   When leaving a dock under sail with the wind blowing the boat back onto the dock, try to set off from the end of the dock. This will let the boat sag to leeward (downwind) without hitting the dock. Make sure the main boom and main sheet are free to run and, as you leave, make sure they do not tangle in cleats or gear on the dock. Push off, and do not pull the sails in until you are clear of the dock.

Leaving a Dock

When you step into your dinghy to sail away from the dock, the factors that come into play are the wind and tide. If both are moving away from the dock, leaving is easy. If the wind and tide are pushing you onto the dock, things get much harder. Typically, you will push off from the dock and start the boat sailing. With luck, the wind won't blow you back against the dock before you get some speed up. Figure 5.1 shows how to get a dinghy away from the dock when the wind is blowing against you. The trick is to start at the very end of the dock.

With a slightly larger boat, the problems increase. Usually there is a boat ahead or astern of you, so you cannot let your boat slide backward; nor can you simply sail out forward. In this case, you might use a spring line to hold the boat in place while you get it ready to sail. Figure 5.2 shows how an aft spring can be used to prevent the boat from sliding backward. With wind blowing parallel to the dock, the idea is to let the boat's bow slide away from the dock while a spring line holds the stern in place. Place fenders aft in case you make contact with the dock, and push the helm toward the dock to help turn the bow away from it. As soon as the bow is pointing outward you can sheet in the mainsail to get speed on the boat, and let go the spring line.

This maneuver can also be used if the boat has an engine and you are leaving the dock under power. If the boat has an inboard engine, your first step (even before starting the engine) is to see that the engine-intake sea-cocks are open. This allows water to flow through the engine to cool it. Start the engine by pressing the ignition button, and then check to see that water is coming out of the exhaust line. This tells you that the engine is being cooled properly.

A spring line can be used to hold the boat alongside while the engine is put astern with the rudder over. As soon as the bow is clear of the boat ahead, put the engine ahead and let go the spring line. Be sure you do not drop the spring line into the water, where it might get sucked into the prop.

Spring lines can also be used to move a boat around a marina or to get it into the right place without using the engine. For example, suppose you want to turn your boat around in a slip. You might use a forward spring to kick the stern outward, and then take a line from the stern quarter to the dock to pull the stern

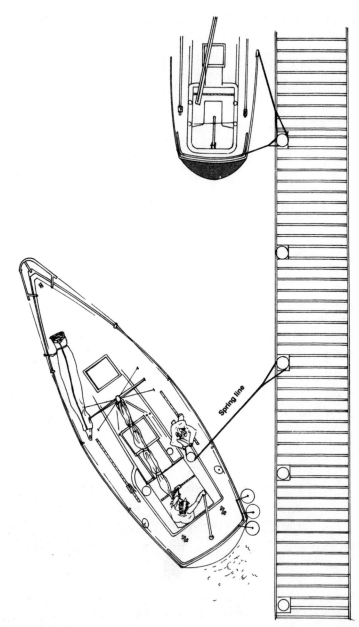

FIGURE 5.2   This technique can be used to get a boat out of a tight space under power. Here a spring line is set up, and the boat is backed down on it. With the helm pulled toward the helmsman (to port), the bow will move away from the dock. As soon as the bow has moved out far enough, the engine should be put ahead and the helm put to starboard (as shown). If the spring line is now let go, the boat is clear of the dock.

around. Note that you will need fenders around the bow to stop it from riding up onto the dock. Figure 5.3 shows you the technique.

In another situation you might have to make a very sharp turn as you leave the dock to get out of the marina. Here a spring line will help pull the bow of the boat around faster than you could expect it to come around under engine power alone. Figure 5.4 shows you how to make the turn.

Quite often you enter a slip bow-first. This may make it difficult to get the boat back out of the slip and out of the marina.

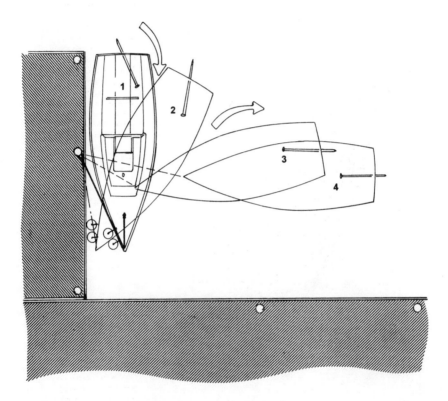

FIGURE 5.3 Using one spring line, a boat can easily be turned around at the dock. In position 1, the dock lines are removed and a forward spring line left on. The helm is put to port and the engine put ahead (or the boat is pushed ahead). Fenders should be placed at the bow to cushion impact with the dock. The boat will move to position 2. At this stage the rudder is put to starboard and the engine reversed. As the boat moves astern, the rudder is centered until the dock line is taut. (You may want to ease the dock line out a little, if space permits.) The boat then reaches position 3.

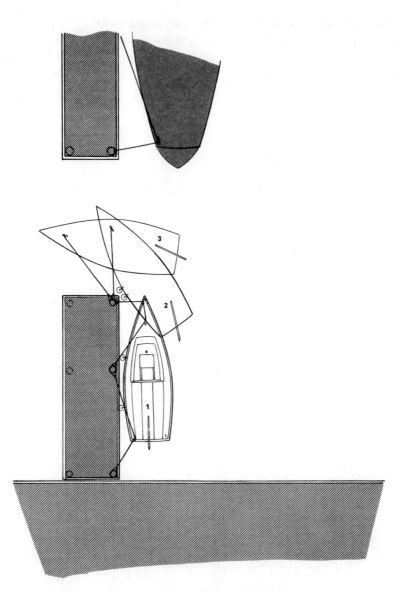

FIGURE 5.4 Spring lines can also be used to get the boat around a tight corner. Here the boat may not be able to negotiate the tight turn, so a spring line is used to pull it around. Use a forward spring attached to the dock-corner bollard and power gently against it. Put the helm to starboard, as in position 2, and put fenders where contact with the dock is likely. Keep powering gently ahead and the boat will gradually swing around the corner to position 3. At this point, the spring can be cast off and the boat can leave the marina.

Figure 5.5 shows you how to back the boat out of a slip using a spring line. Then you can head out to the marina entrance.

When the wind and tide are both moving in the same direction, getting away from the seawall or dock is easy: You simply push

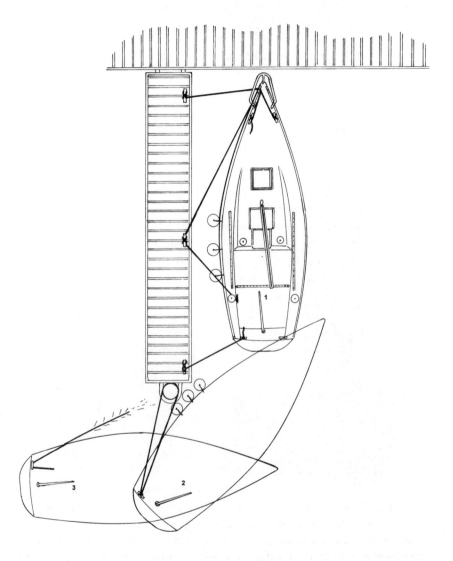

FIGURE 5.5   The same technique is used to turn a boat around a corner and get it out of the slip to face in the right direction to leave the marina. By backing out and using a stern spring, the boat is turned to face the proper direction.

off and let the wind or tidal stream carry you away from the dock. As soon as you are clear, you can start sailing. Difficulties come when the wind is blowing against the tide. This usually makes the waves larger and the conditions a little more bouncy, so keep your fingers clear of the boat and the dock. With wind against tide, you can push off and let the sails draw you clear. Because the boat is moving against the tide, the boat will seem to be moving much more slowly. This helps to give you time to get your thoughts together.

There are many ways of leaving a dock either under power or under sail. You should learn and practice each technique until you are comfortable with it. Then you will have the confidence to bring your boat in and out of a dock without worrying about whether you are going to damage it.

Leaving a Mooring

In many areas your boat will hang off a mooring that you need to leave when you start your sail and pick up again at the end. Letting go the mooring may seem easy: You simply drop the mooring line over the side. But if you try to do this without being properly prepared, you may drift down on another boat or into shallow water. I have done both at one time or another. Your drift will be particularly rapid when the tide is moving in the same direction as the wind. In this case, after letting go the mooring line, you should back the jib, put the helm over, and let the boat come beam-on to the wind. In this position it's easy to trim the mainsail and jib and get the boat going ahead, as shown in Figure 5.6.

Remember to figure out beforehand where your best course will be. For example, in Figure 5.7 leaving the mooring by going to port may be very difficult under sail, because your boat may not have enough way on before it hits another boat. You might want to turn and follow a track Y, or you might try going in the other direction, even though it takes you toward shallower water.

When the wind and tide are moving in opposite directions your job is a little easier, because you can use your sails to control the rate at which you go up- or downtide.

Just like leaving the mooring under sail, leaving under power is fairly easy. Cast off the mooring line and allow the boat to drift

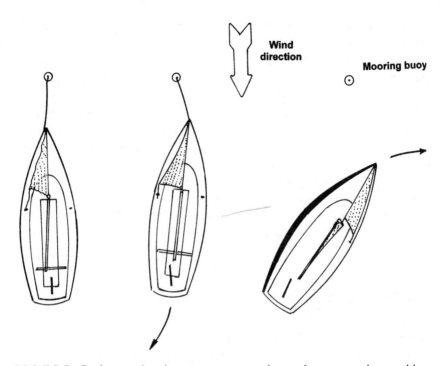

FIGURE 5.6 When leaving a mooring, let go the mooring line and let the boat drop back. Put the helm to starboard and the jib to port to turn the boat to starboard. Once the boat is turned, the sails can be sheeted in and some boat speed gained. Gradually sheet the sails in farther if you need to go to windward, but let the boat get some speed first.

back, or put the engine astern and drop back. Make sure that there is someone on the bow to point to the mooring buoy by holding up one arm to indicate the direction in which it lies. If you neglect to do this, the helmsman, who can't see the buoy from the stern, may accidentally run over it. As soon as you have dropped back far enough to clear the buoy, put the engine ahead and turn sharply right or left to avoid the buoy.

If you want to display gross incompetence, all you need do is to run over your own mooring buoy and tangle the line around your prop. Not only do you have to go over the side to cut the mooring buoy free, but you also have to find a place to moor your boat while you tell the boatyard or marina operator what you have done. Then the boatyard or marina has to retrieve mooring line. You can be

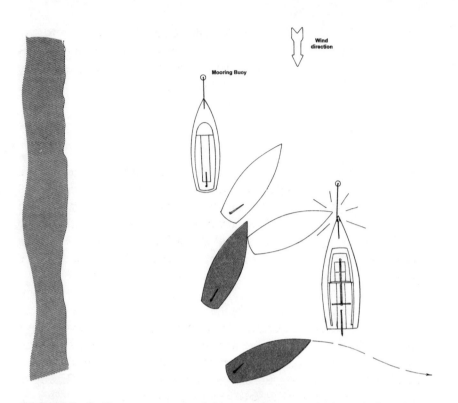

FIGURE 5.7   In a mooring field your options may be limited. If you let go the mooring and try to make a normal turn, you will hit the other boat. In this case, let your boat drop back farther to get clear of the other boat, or drop back and turn the other way, even though you stand a chance of going aground.

sure they will tell every skipper within earshot why they are diving where your boat is supposed to be.

Hoisting Sail

In a dinghy or small boat you will hoist sail before you get under way and leave the dock or mooring. On a larger boat you might leave the dock under power and then hoist sail. No matter how you do it, though, there are some basic rules to follow.

If it's possible, put the boat head-to-wind before hoisting sail. This way the sails will blow down the middle of the boat. Of course, putting the boat head-to-wind may be impossible if it's alongside a dock; you will have to make allowances. Let the rudder and the sheets go, and allow plenty of slack before hoisting sail. In a dinghy that you have to sail off a dock, you may need to put the centerboard and the rudder down before leaving.

Tacking and Gibing

An old adage says, "Gentlemen never sail upwind." Indeed, sailing upwind is hard work. The wind feels stronger, spray comes aboard the boat, the boat heels over, and the crew has to get to one side to keep the boat upright. If you are young and strong, sailing to windward in a dinghy strengthens your stomach muscles. But if you are older, try to do your upwind sailing aboard a bigger boat, where physical strength is not such an important requirement.

As you already know, sailboats cannot sail directly into the wind; they have to sail at an angle to the wind. Then they turn, or tack to sail across the wind on the other angle. To tack, you push the tiller away from you if you are sitting on the weather side (the side nearest to the wind). Remember that tacking is when the bow of the boat passes through the wind as the boat turns. Gibing is when the stern of the boat passes through the wind.

There is a series of orders to give when tacking or gibing that feel awkward when you first start to sail, but let everyone onboard know what is about to happen. The first order for a tack is given by the helmsman, who says, "Standby to tack," or, "Prepare to tack." This lets the crew know that the boat is going to turn. The crew makes sure that the ropes are free to run and that the sails can cross the boat without snagging on anything. A snag can tear a sail.

At the moment of turning the helm the helmsman says, "Tacking," or, "Lee ho." This tells the crew that the boat is going into the turn and that the jib sheet (that is, the line holding the headsail) can be let go. It also tells the crew that it's time to duck, because the boom will cross the centerline of the boat and may hit them on the head if they don't move. (*Warning:* Booms on large boats have been known to kill people who didn't duck in time!) After the crew and the helmsman duck under the boom, they set themselves up on the weather side. Once the boat has settled down, you can continue to sail upwind until it's time to tack again, or until you want to turn and come onto a reach.

Setting Up the Sails to Suit the Wind Strength

Whether your sails are old or new doesn't matter if they are set incorrectly. If the halyard tension is wrong, the sail will not work properly. If the sheet is not positioned right, the sail will not be effective. To learn how to set a sail up properly, start at the dock with the jib.

Some early morning when there is very little wind, hoist the jib while the boat is alongside the dock. Tighten the halyard until vertical creases start to appear in the luff, or leading edge, of the sail, then ease the halyard back until the creases just disappear. Next, pull in the sheet and bisect the angle at the clew, as shown in Figure 5.8. Because the leach, or trailing edge, of the sail is longer than the luff, you will have to adjust the angle downward slightly to get a more vertical pull on the leach. Where the sheet meets the deck is where you should locate the jib sheet fairlead, or track car. The fairlead car is mounted on a track. On boats larger than a dinghy the fairlead, or track car, is moved forward or aft to suit the trim of the sail.

Now go out for a sail, preferably in light winds. Hoist the jib and sheet it in. Go forward and check the luff. Are there vertical lines parallel to the forestay? If so, you should ease the halyard slightly until the lines just disappear. Are there horizontal lines along the luff? Tighten the halyard until they disappear (but make sure that you do not introduce vertical lines). If all the lines have disappeared, the sail is set properly. Figure 5.9 shows this technique.

Now check the telltales along the inside of the luff of the sail. Are they all lifting together? If so, the sail is set properly. If the top one lifts first, it's a sign that the sheet lead is too far aft and the sail is too open at the top; move the lead forward a little. If the bottom telltale lifts first, the foot is too round, and you should move the sheet lead a little farther aft. Figure 5.10 shows the technique.

Be aware that a properly set sail is positioned for a particular wind strength. If the wind increases, the settings will change, and the sail will need to be readjusted. This is why racing sailors work so hard to continually adjust their sails. Cruising sailors who don't worry about getting the best speed out of their boat usually don't need to adjust the sails, except during major wind changes.

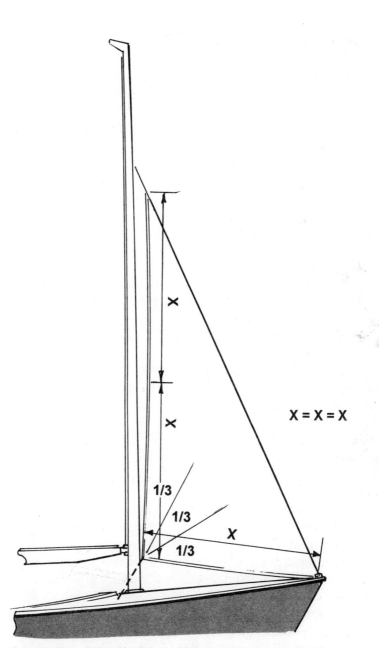

X = X = X

1/3
1/3
1/3

X

FIGURE 5.8   When deciding where to locate the jib fairlead or car, bisect the angle at the clew of the sail and project the sheet to the deck. That's where your fairlead (or car) should go. In this sketch the leach is twice as long as the foot, so the sheet angle is one-third of the clew angle. This is a good place to start when setting up the jib.

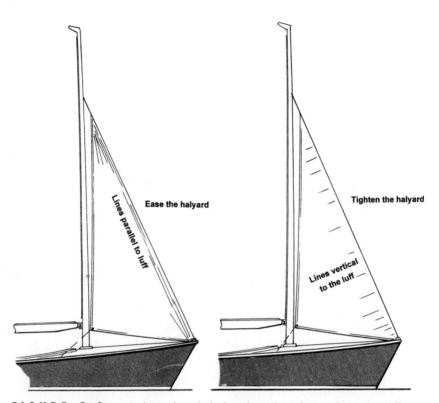

Ease the halyard

Lines parallel to luff

Tighten the halyard

Lines vertical to the luff

FIGURE 5.9   Tighten the jib halyard until no lines along the luff are shown. In (A) lines appear parallel to the luff of the sail. This shows that the halyard is too tight. Easing it will get rid of the lines. In (B) the halyard has been eased too much and lines perpendicular to the luff appear. Tightening the halyard will get rid of these lines.

Now that you've learned about setting the jib, you can work on the mainsail. But before you set the mainsail, take some red or black wool or ribbon and sew a six- to twelve-inch length to each batten pocket. If your dinghy doesn't have a batten pocket, sew two or three lengths to the leach of the sail. If you are sailing on a larger boat, make the woolies or telltales about twelve to eighteen inches long. Installing telltales at each batten pocket will help you trim the sail properly.

As you did with the jib, you should first try to set the mainsail in no wind at the dock. Hoist the sail and tighten the halyard until vertical creases appear. Then slacken the halyard a small amount

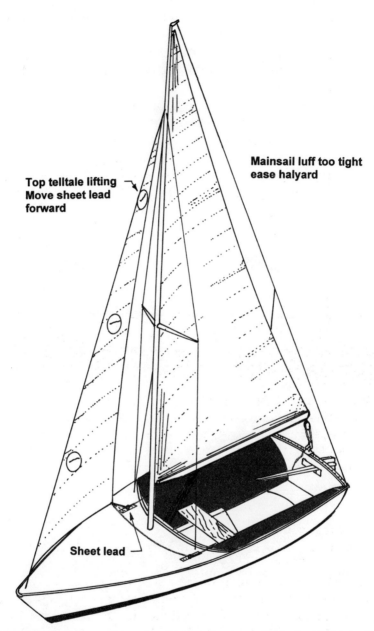

Top telltale lifting
Move sheet lead
forward

Mainsail luff too tight
ease halyard

Sheet lead

FIGURE 5.10   The sail appears to be set correctly, but the top telltales are lifting (standing upright). Moving the sheet fairlead forward will tighten the sail leach and make all the telltales lift together. If the bottom telltales lift first, move the sheet fairlead slightly aft.

until the creases just disappear. Pull the foot along the boom and tighten it so that no horizontal creases are visible.

Now go sailing. If horizontal or vertical creases appear either along the luff or along the foot of the mainsail, you should adjust the boom or halyard tension until they disappear. This may mean that you have to stop the boat and lower the boom to pull the foot out a little more, but that's okay. Just don't stop in a shipping channel.

Once you have the sail shaped properly, you need to adjust the mainsheet so the telltales that you sewed to the luff all stream out aft of the sail, as shown in Figure 5.11. If your boat does not have a traveler (a slide on a track), quite often the top telltale will not set properly; ignore it. If the boat has a traveler, though, adjust it so the boom is close to the centerline of the boat. Its actual position will depend on the type of boat you are sailing. Now look up the leach of the sail from underneath the boom. The bottom two battens should be parallel to the boom, and the upper two battens open a slight angle with the boom. Pull the mainsheet in until the telltales are streaming aft. If the top ones disappear around the back of the sail, you have pulled it in too far, so you should ease it out again. When the sail has no creases and the telltales are streaming aft, the sail is set properly.

Ending Your Sail

You have had your sailing fun, and now it's time to return to the dock or mooring. How do you do it? I have watched novices slam into docks or grab buoys only to have to let go because the helmsman forgot to let go the mainsheet, and the boat kept sailing. I have also seen near misses as a boat sailed toward a mooring, dropped the sails, and was going too slowly to get to the buoy. All these things will happen. Simply chalk them up to experience and try again.

Picking Up a Mooring

When you are picking up a mooring under sail, be cognizant of both tidal-stream and wind directions. You should always try to

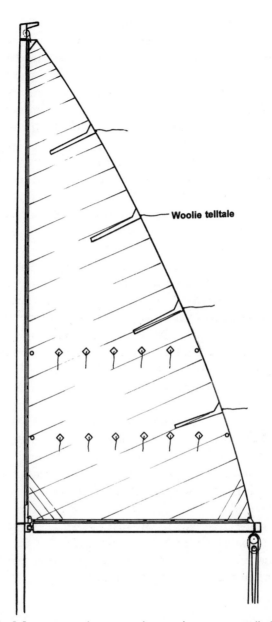

Woolie telltale

FIGURE 5.11   To set the mainsail properly, put some telltales on the battens pockets (these are where you insert the sail "stiffeners"). When the sail is set properly, they will all lift together. Note that some boats sail faster with the top telltale not set properly because of mast turbulence. You will need to learn how your own boat sails.

come into a mooring uptide, unless the wind and tide are moving in the same direction. Coming in uptide takes some speed off the boat and makes it easier to get to the mooring buoy the first time. With wind and tide in the same direction, you should approach the buoy by sailing across them and then rounding up at the last minute, as shown in Figure 5.12. This requires a little practice to ensure that the dinghy is stopped as you arrive at the buoy.

When the wind and tide are against each other, the helmsman's job is much easier. You can run toward the mark (downwind) and reduce sail (drop the mainsail and sail under jib alone). This will slow the boat until it's only just overcoming the speed of the tidal stream. As soon as the buoy is in hand, drop all the sails and make the mooring fast, as shown in Figure 5.13.

If the wind and tide are across your mooring, you will have to modify these basic techniques to get to the mooring. Usually, you will start your approach uptide of the buoy and sail on a broad reach toward the mooring, rounding up at the last moment, as shown in Figure 5.12. It's important not to get too far downwind of the mooring buoy or you will have to beat back to it. In this situation, the boat is approaching the mooring under headsail only, because this sail is easier to let go when the mooring is grabbed. But you should know that under headsail you will make a lot of leeway, which you should allow for. If you have to beat back to the buoy under jib alone, it might take a long time. Notice also that the boat has rounded up just to the side of the buoy. If a crew member misses the buoy, the boat can easily be laid off to starboard and the jib sheeted in fast enough to get some way on again before you drift too far downwind.

In all the mooring situations I've outlined here, it is important to let go or drop your sails just as you reach the buoy. You don't want to be tethered to the buoy with your boat under sail. This can lead to a capsize, or (even worse) the boat could jibe and crack somebody on the head with the boom.

Coming Alongside a Dock

I've watched many boats come alongside, but the most spectacular was a forty-five-footer. The wind was quite strong and blowing the boat away from the dock. The owner, who obviously knew quite a

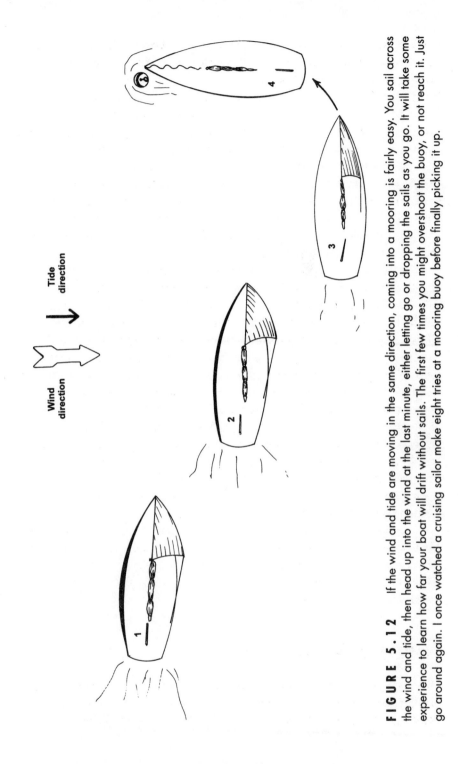

FIGURE 5.12 If the wind and tide are moving in the same direction, coming into a mooring is fairly easy. You sail across the wind and tide, then head up into the wind at the last minute, either letting go or dropping the sails as you go. It will take some experience to learn how far your boat will drift without sails. The first few times you might overshoot the buoy, or not reach it. Just go around again. I once watched a cruising sailor make eight tries at a mooring buoy before finally picking it up.

Wind direction

Tide direction

**Tide
direction**

**Wind
direction**

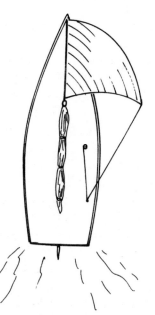

FIGURE 5.13 With the wind against the tide, you should drop the main-sail and proceed under jib only. The tidal stream will slow your boat while you approach the buoy under jib. As soon as you reach the buoy, let go of the jib sheet so that the sail can flap, then drop it or roll it up on the roller-furling gear.

lot about his boat, came in at speed to get the bow secure before it blew off to leeward. A crew member stood in the bow ready with a dock line. As the boat approached the dock, the owner put the engine astern. A great roar followed, and the water frothed under the transom.

When the swirling water settled, the boat was still moving ahead at about five knots. The bowman threw the dock line and snagged a cleat. The stern crew then threw the dock line at a cleat but missed. When the bowman tried to take the load on the line, it snapped. The boat then plowed into the stern of the boat ahead, causing a lot of damage. What happened? The owner's technique was perfectly acceptable, but the nut on the propeller had come loose. When he threw the boat astern, the prop nut dropped off, followed by the propeller itself. A diver found it directly under the stern of the boat.

Coming into a dock can be quite hazardous even if your prop doesn't drop off. When you come alongside for the first time you, should get your boat moving slowly. After all, you don't want to ding your boat, or anyone else's. First, practice in light winds or in relatively calm conditions. Make sure your boat has enough steerage that the rudder can control it, and have extra crew aboard just in case.

The easiest time to come alongside a dock under sail is when the wind is blowing down the dock. You simply bring the boat head-to-wind close to the dock and you have arrived. One thing to remember, though, is to time your approach so that you are coming in slowly. You will need to get spring or stern lines onto cleats on the dock to stop the boat, and at high speeds you can easily break a mooring line or rip a cleat off the dock.

When putting a line on a dock cleat while the boat is still moving, make sure you have a wrap of line around one of the boat's cleats. Ease the line out as the boat comes alongside, and gradually put pressure on the line. Don't have a lot of slack in the line and suddenly tighten it, or you will probably damage something. Don't try to hold the line barehanded while the boat is still moving. Unless you have a small dinghy, you'll either let go the line or hold on—and be dragged over the side! Also make sure you have plenty of fenders out. If you use a spring line to stop the boat, it will come to rest against the dock. Fenders are intended to absorb that impact; they will be crushed, rather than your boat.

Unfortunately, the wind is not often blowing directly down the dock. It might be blowing onto the dock, away from the dock, or across the dock at an angle. You need to use special techniques to enable you to get alongside under these conditions. If the wind is blowing away from the dock, landing gets a little tricky. In this case put the bow in toward the dock, turn, and try to get a stern line ashore. Use two lines to get the boat alongside.

If your boat has a high bow that tends to blow off as you come alongside, get a bow line ashore and leave plenty of slack in it. Allow the bow to move away from the dock and bring the stern in to get a line ashore. Then pull the boat into the dock. This is one of the most difficult operations to perform and usually results in a very inelegant landing.

Coming alongside under power is much easier than without power, because reversing the propeller allows you to stop. When approaching the dock, check for lines over the side before starting the engine. Then, with the engine running, you can easily power up to the dock and put the boat in place whether the wind is blowing onto or away from the dock. Remember that the propeller will usually thrust the stern to port when it is put astern hard, making it easier to bring the stern in toward the dock when the dock is on your port side. When I taught sailing many years ago, we had an old launch with a large slow-speed engine. When that engine was put astern, the stern would kick hard to port. This made it easy to come alongside to port, but almost impossible to dock the boat on the starboard side. Beginners learning to bring the boat in used to do virtually anything to come in portside.

If you have to dock your boat into a space between two other vessels, the job becomes a little harder. Bring the boat alongside the slip and toss lines ashore, then winch the boat into the space. If the space is a lot longer than the boat, you can put either the bow or the stern in and use a spring line to pull the other end in toward the dock.

LEAVING YOUR BOAT

Leaving Your Boat in a Marina

Leaving your boat in a marina is a good option because the boat can be watched over by the marina operator and staff. To tie off a boat in a marina, you should put breast lines at the bow and stern, and two springs to stop the boat moving fore and aft. Quite often you can take a second bow line across the front of the dock and dispense with one of the springs. Figure 5.14 shows how to moor up your boat in a marina.

Leaving Your Boat on a Mooring

Leaving your boat on a mooring requires a different technique. First, check around the bow area to see if there are any sharp edges that might chafe the mooring line. If you find any, round them off. When you are leaving your boat on a mooring, you should also make sure that the mooring lines have some form of chafe protec-

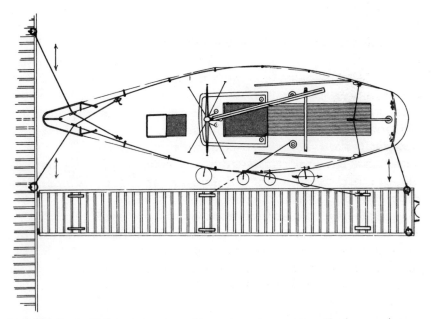

FIGURE 5.14   How to tie off your boat in a marina. The bow and stern breast lines hold the bow and stern in. The aft spring stops the boat from moving forward. The starboard bow breast line is led to another cleat or mooring ring to stop the bow from moving toward the dock and to stop the boat from moving aft. If you cannot install a breast line in this fashion, simply add another spring line (shown dashed). The bow and stern will not move much, because they are held by the breast lines and pivot on the fenders. In storms double up on the dock lines and add extra fenders.

tion on them. Use a bridle so that if one side chafes, there is another to hold your boat. Fasten the bridle eye to both bow cleats and use a thinner line to secure the mooring line on the cleat.

Make sure the mooring is adequate for the weight and size of your boat; check the mooring chain and pennant regularly for signs of wear. If a storm is forecast, remove items such as bimini tops, dodgers, and roller-furling gear so that they will not be destroyed by the wind. (A bimini top is a large umbrellalike structure that shelters the crew from the sun. A dodger is a canvas shelter usually positioned at the front of the cockpit to protect crew from waves and wind coming over the front of the boat. And roller-furling gear is used to roll up the headsail on larger boats. Usually, the headsail is left stored on the roller-furling unit.)

Leaving Your Boat at Anchor

Leaving your boat at anchor has a slightly higher element of risk than the other three options. You should make sure that the anchor is firmly bedded down, and that the boat is not moving. This might take an hour or two of observation before you go away and leave the boat for a week. If you are sure that the anchor is bedded in properly and that the anchor line is protected from chafe, tie it off. You can also clamp the anchor chain by using what's called a devil's claw—a device, usually metal, used to clamp the chain tightly so that it will not run out if it comes loose. (It's also known as a chain clamp, or anchor clamp.)

How long you can safely leave your boat at anchor will depend on the weather, the depth of water, tides, and other factors. But there is no reason your boat cannot stay at anchor while you're away—provided that the ground tackle is sufficiently heavy.

Leaving Your Boat Alongside

Leaving your boat alongside a dock or seawall can get tricky, depending on the rise and fall of tides. In the Channel Islands, for example, the rise and fall of tide can be twenty or more feet. If you choose to leave your boat alongside under these conditions, make sure your dock lines are long enough to hold the boat when the tide is out. Quite often you will find that the boat will float a considerable distance from the dock wall when the tide is high. This is fine, as long as you have adequate fenders to prevent chafe when the boat is alongside.

It's when the wind is blowing your boat against the dock wall that problems arise. When this happens, you should consider a breast line to keep the boat off the dock. Use your dinghy to carry the anchor out, and set a buoyed anchor line, known as a breast line, to keep the boat off the wall. Gently lower your anchor into the dinghy and drop it abeam of the boat. Make sure the anchor is marked with a buoy so other vessels know where it is. Tighten the breast line to hold the boat off the seawall.

These are some of the basic boat-handling techniques you will need to master before you go out in your own boat. You will probably get to practice a lot of them at a sailing school or with a small boat before you try them with your own larger boat. Every time you come into a dock or mooring, figure out where the wind and tide are coming from and get yourself set up to bring the boat in under sail, even if you have an engine. If the engine fails, you will still be ready.

CHAPTER 6

KNOTS

You cannot set the sails properly without tying the sheets to the sails; nor can you cleat a line off without using the right method. First you need to know about knots and understand cleat tying, which is really just another method of tying a knot. You can't use just any old knot when sailing. You have to use one that can be tied, relied on to hold, and untied easily. Untying a knot is very important. If you had to cut the line every time you wanted to change a sheet, you would soon end up with no lines left. The importance of using the right knot is illustrated by the following vignette.

We were out sailing and, as we came near the leeward mark, we were getting ready for a spinnaker takedown. One of the crew quickly took a couple of turns and a half hitch around a cleat with the foreguy, then turned to the afterguy. As we came to the mark and the boat squared away, the skipper called for the pole to be pulled aft. The person on the afterguy wound it aft on a winch—without letting go the foreguy. A few minutes later a crewman tried to undo the foreguy. The half hitch had pulled so tight that it was impossible to move. We finally had to cut it away.

The correct way to cleat off a line is to wrap the line around the cleat, as shown in Figure 6.1, and finish by taking a turn

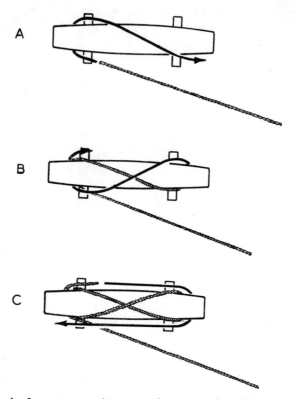

FIGURE 6.1   To put a line on a cleat correctly, take a wrap around the end of the cleat (A). Bring the line over the top and under the other end, then double it back over the top of the cleat and around the end (B). Finish with a wrap around the base of the cleat (C). If the cleat has to carry a heavy load, a second wrap over and under the ends with a final wrap around the cleat will be required. Never put a half hitch on a cleat. You may not be able to get it undone in a hurry.

around the bottom of the cleat. This will hold in virtually all circumstances, as long as the line is sized to suit the cleat. Where a line is taken from a winch to a cleat, the load on the cleat is really quite light if there are at least three turns around the winch. If the load is likely to be heavy, another crossover on the cleat is necessary. But beware a line that is too small for the cleat; you will have problems. Cleats work best when the line is of the correct diameter. In general, the cleat should be eight times the line's diameter.

Cleats were originally developed by sailors to hold lines that were meant to be released quickly. If you go aboard an old working ship, you will never see a line tied off tightly; every line is stowed in such a way that it can be released instantly. The vagaries of the wind and sea being what they are, sailors never know when a line might be needed.

Old-time sailors had a vast repertoire of knots. They knew how to put a temporary line on a spar, a mast, or another line; what knot to use to tie off a sheet; and how to coil a line. For example, a square knot, sometimes called a reef knot (see Figure 6.2), is rarely used for anything other than tying in the reef lines on a sail. The reason is that if you pull on one side of the knot, it collapses. In fact, a well-known way to untie a reef knot is to pull on one side. (See parts D and E in Figure 6.2.) This causes the knot to turn into a pair of half hitches, which can easily be slid off the line.

Because it collapses so easily, you should never use a square knot to tie two lines of different sizes. When a strain is put on the lines, the thicker line will straighten and the knot will collapse. The *Ashley Book of Knots* claims that more lives have been lost by using the reef knot to tie two lines together than any other half-dozen knots combined. Where you want to tie two lines together, you should use a sheet bend. This looks like a reef knot, except that the last tuck of the knot is taken under itself rather than back under the other side. This stops the knot from pulling apart when a load is put on it. If one line is very thick, use a double sheet bend—that is, take the thin line twice around the thick line before tucking it back under itself.

The sheet bend looks something like a bowline, which is the most commonly seen knot aboard boats today (besides the snarl that most lines develop if they don't have both ends tied off). A bowline is a relatively easy knot to tie. A simple mnemonic for tying

FIGURE 6.2   A square or reef knot should be used for only a limited number of jobs, as it can easily collapse. Pull on the ends (D) and (E) to collapse the knot into two half hitches, which will then slide off the line.

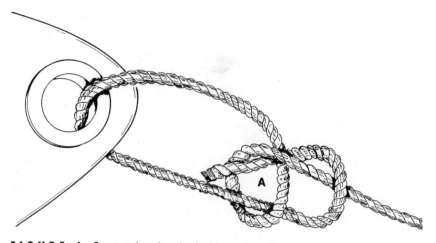

FIGURE 6.3 A bowline looks like a sheet bend but is tied with one part of the line. (The procedure to tie it is easily remembered with the mnemonic, "Through the hole, around the tree, and back down the hole.") To tie it, make the loop (A is in the middle of it), pass the line through the sail, back through the loop (the hole), then around the standing part (the tree), and back through the loop (the hole) again.

it is: "Make a loop, then send the rabbit up the hole, around the tree, and back down the hole." Figure 6.3 shows you how the knot is tied.

Another useful knot is the rolling hitch. If you ever have to move a sheet or guy from one winch to another, use a rolling hitch. To tie this knot, take several turns around the guy with a thinner line (make sure the thin line can carry the load of the larger one).

Guy

FIGURE 6.4 A rolling hitch is used to tow logs, secure one line to another, or take the load while a sheet or guy is being transferred to another winch. To tie it, take four to six wraps around the line or object to be secured. Then secure the end with a half hitch, as shown. As the load comes onto the new line, the knot will twist, but if it is made properly it will not slip.

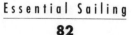

Finish the hitch off with a half hitch on the end, as shown in Figure 6.4. As the strain is eased off the winch, the rolling hitch will tighten and hold the guy. You can then easily move the guy and take the strain on a new winch before removing the rolling hitch.

On one offshore trip some years ago I watched in dismay as the end of the halyard disappeared up the mast. It was then that I learned how far it is to the masthead while the boat is at sea, and how useful a stopper knot can be. This knot can be made in a number of variations. The simplest is the thumb (or overhand) knot, which is tied as shown in Figure 6.5. If you wrap the turns a second time, you will have a blood knot, so called because it was once tied in the ends of a cat-o'-nine-tails and drew blood when the lash was used. If the turns are wrapped a third time, the knot becomes a triple or threefold overhand knot, which the *Ashley Book of Knots* says is also called a French knot. But most sailors will use a figure-eight knot, as shown in Figure 6.6. This knot was around before Admiral Lord Nelson was a midshipman (1771) and may date back to the days of the Spanish Armada. If the line is slightly small, however, a figure-eight knot can get jammed in a sheave.

A great knot for holding a reefing line to the end of the boom is a timber hitch, as shown in Figure 6.7. To make this knot, take a turn around the boom, loop the reefing line around itself, and then wrap it around the part under the boom several times. As the strain comes onto the line, the timber hitch pulls tight and will not

FIGURE 6.5   Stopper knots should be used to stop line from disappearing up the mast or over the stern. The simplest is the overhand knot. If two turns are made around the standing part, the knot becomes a blood knot.

Knots

FIGURE 6.6 A figure-eight knot is one of the most commonly used stopper knots.

undo. As soon as it is time to shake the reef out, though, let the load off; the hitch falls apart.

The best knots used on boats are those that hold tightly but can easily be undone when needed. For this reason, you should learn to tie more than a bowline, and learn where each knot is best suited.

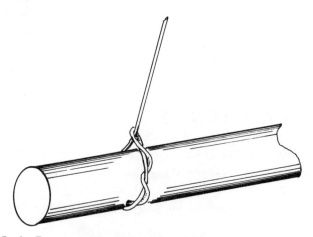

FIGURE 6.7 A timber hitch is one of the best knots you can use to tie a reefing line to the end of the boom. Under strain it will hold until the line breaks, but once the load is off, the knot collapses easily. To tie it, take the reef line around the boom and then around itself. Wrap the end around the loop on the boom three or more times, and take up the tension on the line.

CHAPTER 7

WHERE AM I?

On land, you buy a road map to show you the way. Similarly, for traveling at sea there are maps known as charts, although there are no roads or exit signs. You have to find your way using the available equipment for navigation, such as compasses, GPS (Global Positioning System), and loran C (long-range navigation). To get started, you need to learn the basics of navigation.

BASIC CONCEPTS IN NAVIGATION

Because there are no yellow lines painted on the ocean, you must determine for yourself which direction to sail. You must also determine the distance you have to travel, how fast you are going, and how much water is under the boat. All these things are basic to navigation.

Direction

You navigate between buoys or between harbors by sailing along a course. When you sail across an ocean or to some far-off place, your course becomes a rhumb line. Strictly speaking, this is a line drawn on the earth's surface that crosses all the meridians at the same angle. The term *rhumb* comes from a French word meaning "compass point," so a boat that is sailing the rhumb is following a compass point. (In some sailing communities the term *rhumb line* has come to mean any course ruled on a chart, but its true use is for offshore sailing.)

Mercator charts are based on the Mercator projection, which places the meridians of latitude and longitude at right angles to each other no matter where on the earth's surface they are. Mercator projections are used on most charts today. When drawn on a Mercator chart, a rhumb line is a straight line, but it's not necessarily the shortest route between two points. The shortest course is usually a great circle route, which appears curved on a Mercator chart.

Sometimes it's impossible to sail along the rhumb line. For example, when your destination is dead upwind, the boat must sail along a heading and make a course made good. This is like sailing a regular course but going in a zigzag fashion to get there, as shown in Figure 7.1. The course along which you are sailing is known as the ship's heading and is expressed in degrees or by a compass point. For example, the helmsman might say, "I am steering southwest," or, "We are heading 250 degrees."

The heading of the boat is not the only direction you might express when finding your way in the ocean. If you see another boat, you might check its position to make sure you are not on a collision course. If there are a number of boats nearby, you might give each vessel's direction by referring to its position relative to yours.

For instance, if a boat is approaching from the port bow, the skipper might say that it's "fine on the port bow." Someone else might say, "The boat is at eleven o'clock." Another way of saying the same thing is to assume your boat's bow is due north and give a bearing to the other boat as 350 degrees. All these options are shown in Figure 7.2.

If you want to give an accurate bearing to an object, you should include both its bearing and its distance. In other words, you might say that the Hatteras lighthouse bears 270 degrees and is ten miles away. You can also give an object's position relative to your position and the wind. A boat directly off your starboard

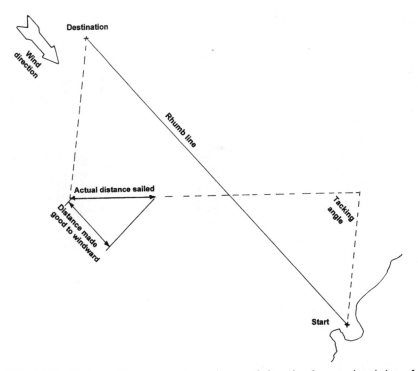

FIGURE 7.1 You may not be able to sail directly along a rhumb line if the wind is against you. In this case, the distance you travel toward your destination is known as the distance made good. If you use a GPS, it will give you a distance known as cross-track error, which tells you how far you are from the rhumb line.

beam, then, may be abeam to windward or abeam to leeward, depending on which side it's on.

Distance

Distance at sea is given as nautical miles from an object. A nautical mile is one degree of latitude. Because the earth is an oblate spheroid rather than a perfectly round ball, a nautical mile varies slightly according to the latitude at which you are sailing, but it's assumed to be the mean of a degree of latitude at the pole and at the equator. Thus it measures 6,076.2 feet (usually rounded off to 6,080 feet)—as opposed the land mile, which measures 5,280 feet. In this

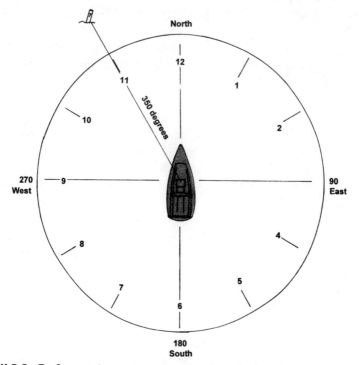

FIGURE 7.2   A bearing can be given from the boat by assuming that the bow is at twelve o'clock or due north. The bearing shown here may be given as eleven o'clock, 350 degrees, or north by northwest; 350 degrees is the most accurate reference.

day of accurate GPS units you are probably better off using 6,076 feet rather than rounding up, although it will make only a slight difference in your position.

Speed

The unit of speed at sea is the knot, defined as one nautical mile per hour. If a boat is traveling at ten knots, it's moving at ten nautical miles per hour or 11.52 land miles per hour.

Speed may also be given relative to an object. For example, the navigator might say the boat is moving past that lighthouse at twelve knots. This speed is the vessel's speed plus that of the tidal current. If the tidal current is two knots moving in the same direction as the vessel, the boat's actual speed is ten knots. If the tidal current is against the boat, on the other hand, the boat would have to be making fourteen knots to maintain a speed past the lighthouse of twelve knots. As I mentioned earlier, the speed at which the vessel is moving relative to a fixed point is also known as speed over the ground (SOG).

Depth

For a car trip all you need to know is direction, distance, and speed of travel, but in a boat there is one other critically important factor. Is the water deep enough for you to sail in? In America *feet* or *fathoms* (one fathom is six feet) is still the standard term used to express water depth. In Europe *meters* is now used, although many charts still show feet and fathoms. All measurements of the same depth are connected by an isobath or depth contour.

Depth contours can be a handy navigation tool if you're in thick fog and cannot check where you are. On one cruise we were stuck offshore in thick fog. Our DR (dead reckoning, or plotted) position put us just off the entrance to the harbor, but the fog was so thick that we could not see our way in. The navigator picked up on the fact that there was a dredged channel where the depth contour changed from twenty-two feet to forty feet. We navigated our way into the harbor by motoring along the edge of the depth contour until we sighted the harbor entrance buoy to one side of the channel.

READING THE COMPASS

A compass is used to steer a course. There are several types of compasses, the magnetic compass being the best known. But gyroscopic compasses, which are used on larger vessels, and electronic compasses (often known as fluxgate compasses) are becoming increasingly popular.

Magnetic Compasses

In its simplest form a magnetic compass consists of a disk floating in a sphere of alcohol, which allows the compass card to be tilted to any angle. The disk is divided into 360 degrees, comprising four cardinal points (N, S, E, and W), and four half-cardinal points (NE, SE, NW, and SW). There are twenty-four other labeled subdivisions, also known as points. This gives a total of thirty-two points on the compass. (In earlier days sailors "boxed" the compass by naming each of the thirty-two points; a ship that made a 360-degree turn was said to have "boxed" the compass.)

Magnetic compasses suffer from two problems that may distort your course. The first is deviation, which is the error caused if ferrous metal or electrical wiring is near the compass. Always check your safety harness clip with a magnet, for example, to make sure it does not affect the compass when you are helming. Ferrous metal objects can cause enormous problems if they are near a magnetic compass.

Some years ago I was delivering a boat from Portland Harbor to Portsmouth along the southern coast of England—a distance of about eighty miles. We set sail from Portland and the fog closed in, cutting visibility to about one mile. We sailed around Anvil Point and set a course for the Needles light, intending to sail up the Solent and into Portsmouth. Somewhere during the trip somebody placed a tin can next to the compass. When we expected to see the Needles lighthouse, we saw nothing. Indeed, we saw nothing for another hour, and we were getting a little worried because we were heading for an area of strong tidal streams and lots of shallow water. Finally, we glimpsed a light way off to our port and turned to head toward it. Instead of the Needles light, which was an occulting light (one that's on longer than it is off), we saw St. Catherine's Light off the southern tip of the Isle of Wight. We were off course by about eight miles. The can on the binnacle had caused the compass to swing slightly and put us several miles off course. We finally sailed around the Isle of Wight and into Portsmouth Harbor, which increased our journey by several hours.

Deviation varies according to the course of the vessel and also from boat to boat. It's found by swinging the compass. To do this, the vessel is swung through 360 degrees while the compass position is accurately recorded relative to a known object—for example, the sun. This exercise, which is performed by a compass adjuster, results in a deviation card that you should keep near your chart table or compass. When you plot a course, add or subtract the deviation according to the card.

The other problem with magnetic compasses is variation. A magnetic compass doesn't point directly to the North Pole, but to a magnetic pole. The location of the magnetic pole varies yearly and according to the position of the observer on the earth's surface. Generally it is given on the chart for the year of publication, along with any yearly increase or decrease. Variation is named east or west, depending on whether the magnetic pole is east or west of the true pole position.

Gyroscopic Compasses

A gyroscopic compass is electronically driven and always points to the true North Pole. It is large and mostly used on bigger vessels, rather than on yachts.

Fluxgate Compasses

Fluxgate compasses are small electronic compasses that point to true north. Usually, with the push of a button the compass will add in the variation to give you magnetic north. Because they do not rely on a spinning card, these are very popular as handheld and autopilot compasses.

FIXING YOUR POSITION

"The DR was three miles ahead of the GPS, which didn't agree with loran at all. How I found the harbor in the fog I'll never know." This confusion happened to a friend of mine on a cruise he took along the coast of Maine. Apparently, the three different methods he was using to fix his position were all different, and he had a hard time deciding which one to believe. Learning to fix a boat's position is a critical part of learning to sail larger boats. At all times you must keep track of the exact position of your boat.

Dead Reckoning

The need to repeatedly "fix" a boat's position isn't obvious to beginning sailors. They don't realize that when out of sight of land, a boat's course can be altered by factors such as a tidal stream, the wind angle, leeway, the helmsman, and even by compass error. Helmsmen or navigators may not realize that the boat isn't on the rhumb line until they get a fix.

To fix a boat's position, take a bearing on a light, or some other identifiable feature. You'll need two bearings that cross at about ninety degrees to fix your position, but three is even better. To aid in locating the boat's current position, keep constant track of the vessel's past positions. Keeping a complete log of where you have already sailed is known as dead reckoning.

Taking a Bearing

The technique is quite simple. Using a handheld compass (remember to have it swung when the boat's main compass is swung), sight over the top of it at an object on shore. Read the object's bearing from the compass, and record it. Take another bearing from another object; again record it. Then find the location of the objects on the chart and draw the bearing line from each object. Where the two lines cross is your boat's position.

Global Positioning System and Loran C

One race back in the mid-1970s involved crossing the English Channel in a thick fog late at night. I watched the navigator sitting at the dimly lit chart table wearing a pair of earphones while he slowly rotated an antenna. After a few minutes of rotating it back and forth, he would take a compass bearing and plot it. Then he'd take another bearing, and another, until he was happy that our position compared reasonably well with the DR position. At that time it all seemed like black magic.

The navigator I was watching was using a method of fixing a boat's position called Radio Direction Finding (RDF). Radio beacons around the coastline transmitted a constant signal on a given frequency. By tuning an antenna on the boat, you could locate the position of the beacon and plot it on your chart; one or two more beacons gave you your position. Radio Direction Finding was still in use as late as 1980, but today it's an antiquated technology.

We now live in an age of satellites and instant communication. For ninety-nine dollars every boat can have a handheld Global Positioning System (GPS) receiver from Magellan, and prices are certain to drop even lower. Using this receiver, a GPS signal is obtained from satellites. Most GPS receivers require a minimum of three to twelve satellites to give an accurate location. GPS gives you a readout of latitude and longitude that can be plotted on a chart. Instantly you have your position. No longer do you need to sight land, the stars, or the sun to find where you are. However, for military reasons the government degrades GPS signals so they will be accurate only to within about three hundred feet. A more up-to-date system, Differential Global Positioning System (DGPS), is reputed to be accurate to within ten feet or less. This system uses additional land stations to increase the accuracy of the satellite signal. As more accurate stations are added, you will be able to locate your position to within five feet.

The next step up from a handheld GPS receiver is a GPS plotter. These can also be handheld or fitted in the boat. A plotter shows a chart of the area in which the boat is sailing and the GPS position of the boat. Plotters use different styles of charts, so ask for advice when purchasing one. (See Plotting a Cruise Electronically on page 101.)

Loran C is another electronic system used to plot a boat's position; it uses a chart with an overlaid loran grid to give you an accurate position. The loran signal is transmitted over land from shore-based loran stations. There is some talk of it being phased out in the near future and the stations closed, but many sailors and boaters want it to continue. Inaccuracies do occur where the loran signal crosses over bodies of land and water, as well as where the loran grid lines cross at an acute angle (near Bermuda, for instance).

On a larger boat you should have both GPS and loran; there may come occasions when satellites aren't available, or your boat isn't in a location to receive both signals.

UNDERSTANDING CHARTS

On a sail a few years ago I could not find the chart for the harbor we were entering. I asked the boat's owner where it might be. He said, "I don't have one. I didn't expect to come here on this trip." We had no idea where the marina we were supposed to moor in was, or even the location of the main channel. We ended up using a large-scale chart with very little information on it. This was a lesson in the importance of carrying not just charts of major areas, but also small-scale charts of harbors, rivers, and other places where you may end up.

Charts are the road maps of the sea. In order to know where you are going at sea you'll need a chart, and then you'll need to understand the markings on the chart. A typical one will have a black border, with the chart number in the lower right and upper left corners. Next to the number is the area covered by the chart—for example, Cape Hatteras to Cape Sable, or Narragansett Bay. Listed under the title of the chart is the scale, such as 1:40,000. If you look at the edge of the chart, you'll see latitude and longitude numbers. Using these numbers you can position the chart accurately in its place in the world. Also along the bottom of the chart is a note telling you in which units the depth measurements are given. On most American charts they are given in feet or fathoms, but today most of the rest of the world uses meters. Also check the lower left corner of the chart. Here you will see the date when the chart was last updated. If the date is more than one year old, you should get your local *Notice to Mariners* to update the chart.

On most small-scale charts the eighteen- or twenty-foot isobath (depth contour) is shown as a dotted line, with all shallower areas shown in blue. On larger-scale charts the ten-fathom isobath is usually shown dotted, and shallower areas are colored blue.

If you look carefully at the chart you can see that a lit buoy is depicted with a small red diamond coming from its top. Under the diamond is a short definition of the light's characteristics. For example, Beavertail light at the southern end of Conanicut Island in Rhode Island (at 71 degrees 24.0 minutes longitude and 41 degrees 26.0 minutes latitude) shows "Fl 6s 64 ft 15M." Since no color is given, you can assume the light is white. Fl 6s means that it flashes every six seconds. The light stands sixty-four feet above the chart datum (mean low water), and it has a range of fifteen miles.

You should familiarize yourself with the characteristics of lights and buoys in your area to make piloting easier. Some navigators draw the ranges of lights on the chart to help estimate when they are likely to become visible. If you are going to spend a lot of time sailing at night, you might want to get a light list, which is available from any chart supplier. A light list gives you information about all the lights in any particular area.

On small-scale charts you will also notice areas of land with height contours marked. These provide you an idea of the topography of the land as you sail into a harbor. Along the shoreline such prominent features as high chimneys, bridges, and water tanks are noted. You can use these points to take a bearing to help find your position. (When taking bearings, don't take them from buoys. Buoys move with the tide, and your bearing may be incorrect.) For example, given the Beavertail light's height of sixty-four feet and fifteen-mile visibility, you could see it and take a bearing on it before you could see the buoy just to its southwest.

Some charts outline prohibited areas in purple. These areas are generally noted, and you should make sure you read the warnings. Off San Diego, for instance, there are areas where unexploded munitions were dumped. You should obviously not anchor in these areas.

Over all of the areas of a chart that are covered by the sea you will find numbers and letters. The numbers represent the depth of water at that point. These measurements are taken at mean low water, which may not be low water at the time you are in the area. They are noted in feet or fathoms, so check on the chart to make sure you're aware of the difference. (A fathom, as noted, is six feet.) Letter abbreviations tell you the type of bottom in an area. For example, *hrd* stands for "hard sand," *rks* for "rocks," and *sh* for "shale."

Dashed lines show the edges of dredged channels or channels that large ships are likely to travel. These channels are usually well buoyed. By law, small-boat sailors should give way to any large vessel in such a channel. Also, you should not anchor in any channel, dredged or otherwise.

Another feature on a chart is a compass rose. This tells you how to orient the chart relative to true or magnetic north. Most compass roses have a circle showing true north and a second circle showing the magnetic north in the year the chart was made. There will also be a note telling you how much variation you can expect to see each year. On one chart I was looking at recently, the variation was fifteen degrees in the year the chart was printed, and it changed at a rate of three minutes per year.

THE BUOYAGE SYSTEM IN THE U.S.

At least twice on each cruise—the beginning and the end—you must navigate through a harbor. To guide you, buoys and other markers are provided by the U.S. Coast Guard. These are laid out to follow the system of buoyage in use in the area where you are sailing. In U.S. coastal waters the lateral system is used. Inland areas use the inland waterway buoyage system. In Europe the cardinal system is in use. Navigation using buoys and landmarks is known as pilotage, and requires a thorough understanding of the buoyage system in use.

When you enter a U.S. harbor, the first buoy you see is the entrance buoy, which may be red or green. If it's red, you should keep it on your starboard (right-hand) side. This buoy will have an even number painted on it (usually the first red buoy is number 2). It will have a red light, and the light's flashing sequence will be marked on the chart. (An easy way to remember on which side to pass a red buoy is "red, right, returning." In other words, keep red buoys on your right when you are returning to harbor.) The buoys in a typical harbor entrance are shown in Figure 7.3.

On your left as you enter a harbor should be a green buoy with an odd number painted on it, often number 1. It will usually flash with a green light, although some older green buoys may still have a white one. (Refer to a chart for the color and sequence.) Buoys at the entrance to a harbor have the lowest numbers; the numbers progress upward as you proceed. Also, as you go farther into the harbor and the water gets shallower, channel buoys will change to red nuns on your right and green cans on your left, as shown in Figure 7.4. These may or may not be lit; usually they are lit where there is a bend in the channel. Farther along, as the channel gets even shallower, nuns change to posts with day marks on them, as shown in Figure 7.5. The one on your right will be a red triangle and the one on your left will be a green square. Day marks don't usually have lights unless they are the first of the series.

Where a channel splits, you will see that the buoys, cans, nuns, and day marks all have two colors, with the color at the top indicating which side of the mark is the preferred channel. If the preferred channel is to the port side, the junction buoy, nun, or

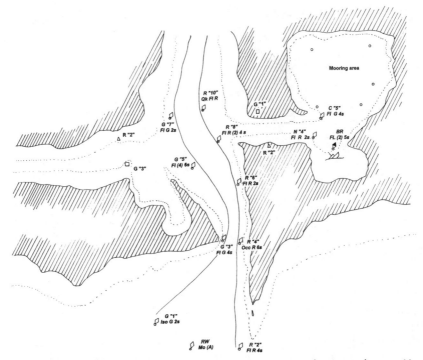

FIGURE 7.3 A port entry showing the layout of various buoys. You should check your chart for information about your harbor. If the data about the buoy is in italics, it means that the buoy is floating. If the numeral is in "quotes," it means that it is marked on the buoy. *R* stands for red, *G* for green, *Y* for yellow. Yellow buoys have yellow lights and are special marks showing anchorages, traffic separation zones, fishnets, and so on. A yellow day mark is diamond shaped rather than the square or triangle of channel top marks. Midchannel buoys may be red and white, red and green, or green and red. The topmost color shows in which direction the main channel lies. For example, a green top shows that the buoy should be left kept on the port side, and that the preferred channel is to the right. If the top color is red, the preferred channel is to the left. Midchannel markers are not cans or nuns, but are spherical with segmented colors, while day marks are octagonal with vertically striped colors.

Regulatory marks such as speed restrictions or no-wake zones are white with orange stripes.

Wreck or isolated danger buoys have a black top, along with a characteristic flashing white group. You should stay well clear of such a mark, because the tide may carry the buoy some distance away from the danger.

For midchannel buoys, *Mo* means that the buoy gives the Morse signal A (short flash–long flash) in white light. The buoy will also have a sound signal.

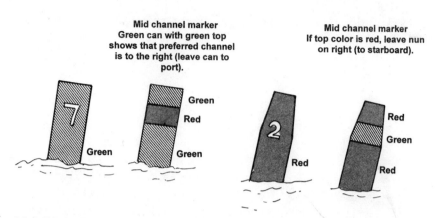

FIGURE 7.4 Cans and Nuns. Cans are square and green, while nuns have a tapered top and are red. Cans and nuns may also be used as midchannel markers. In this case the topmost color tells you on which side the preferred channel lies.

triangular day mark will have a red top and a black or green lower portion. If the preferred channel is to starboard, the buoy, can, or square day mark will have a green top. Lights on junction markers feature interrupted quick flashes.

When you leave a harbor, the sequence is exactly the opposite, with square green day marks on your right, red triangles on

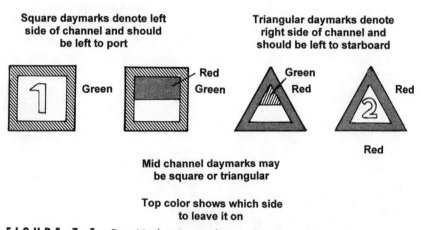

FIGURE 7.5 Day Marks. Green day marks are square and show the left side of the channel when you enter the harbor. Red day marks are triangular and show the right side of the channel when you enter the harbor.

your left. They give way to green cans and red nuns, and then to buoys.

PLANNING YOUR TRIP

Suppose you want to sail from Bridgeport harbor in Connecticut to Newport, Rhode Island. You first lay out your course on a chart and figure out where you wish to be at particular times. For example, you might want to stop overnight or fish a little along the way, or you might decide to detour to Block Island. So you plot how long it might take to make these side trips and determine a time to arrive at your destination.

When you leave on your trip, your planning has already told you how much time it will take and when you expect to get to your destination. It's always good practice to leave a copy of your itinerary with a friend ashore. If you don't arrive by six or eight hours after your estimated time of arrival (ETA), he or she can alert the emergency services.

Plotting a Cruise on a Paper Chart

How do you make out a trip plan like this one? The first step in plotting a cruise is to get a chart of the area in which you intend to sail. For this trip you will need charts of Long Island Sound (Charts 12363 Western Part and 12354 Eastern Part), Block Island Sound (Chart 13205), and Narragansett Bay (Chart 13221), which includes Newport, Rhode Island). You can buy these charts singly from any chandlery, such as Armchair Sailor in Newport, or as a pack from one of the chart kit manufacturers. The typical cost for a single chart is about $14.95. The chart kit required for this trip is New York to Nantucket and costs around ninety-nine dollars, but it includes all the small-scale charts you might require for any harbor between these two locations. Figure 7.6 depicts your course.

In addition to these charts you will need a set of tide tables, which can be found in books such as *Reed's Nautical Almanac* and in periodicals (such as *Soundings*) that publish the tide table for the month for a number of local ports. Tide tables and charts are also available in electronic form if you are up to speed with computers.

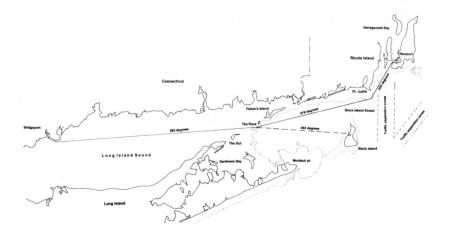

FIGURE 7.6 Using a chart (or series of charts) to plot a course. (This course is condensed from three charts.) Small-scale charts are used to navigate out of the Bridgeport harbor and into Newport Harbor. The dashed line shows the course to Block Island should you decide to go there instead of Newport.

With the appropriate charts and tide tables in front of you, you can begin to lay out your course. From Bridgeport you head east on a course of 083 degrees toward the exit from Long Island Sound. This means you pass through a narrow outlet, either the Race or Plum Gut, and head to Rhode Island. Because the tide flows very strongly through both the Race and Plum Gut (up to four knots), you should plan your trip to pass through either narrow passage when the tide is flowing eastward, the same direction you are heading. Trying to sail through the Race when the tide is against you can be an exercise in frustration. I have seen boats anchored just behind Plum Island for six hours until the tide changes. On this trip you will also cross ship channels, so you will need to exercise caution.

Because of the bottleneck at the Race, check the tide tables to see what time the tide is flowing outward on the day of your trip. Your hypothetical cruise is scheduled for July 1, 1999, so you can see from the tide tables that the tidal stream is strongest going outward or eastward at 2 P.M. (remember to add in an hour for Daylight Saving Time). You want to be going with it at this time. If you assume that the boat will make six knots toward the Race, and that the tide will add an average of three knots to your speed for two hours before you get to the Race, you can estimate a starting time.

The distance is 47.5 miles from Bridgeport to the Race, and for the last two hours you'll be making nine knots over the bottom (totaling 18 miles). This leaves 29.5 miles over which you'll be making about six knots. By dividing the distance by your speed you'll get a time of just under five hours. Thus in order to get to the Race by 2 in the afternoon, you should leave Bridgeport at 7 A.M.

Once you're through the Race, the sail to Newport is fairly easy. You'll head along a course of 078 degrees for 17.7 miles to Point Judith, which should take just under three hours. At the Point Judith light you'll make a turn onto a heading of 025 degrees toward Newport. This leg is only eleven miles, so you will make it to Newport within two hours of rounding the buoy at Point Judith, for an arrival time of about 7 P.M. However, there will be some tide against you as you head into Newport; this will delay your ETA slightly. On a summer day the wind is typically out of the south or southwest, and the sail along the Rhode Island shoreline will be a reach with a run into Newport. Once in Newport, you can partake of one of the fine restaurants in the town and relax after an enjoyable sail.

Plotting a Cruise Electronically

Another way to work out a passage is to use one of the electronic navigation programs available these days. All these programs show a chart on the screen that looks just like a paper chart. Although you can link an electronic chart with a GPS to keep a running fix on your boat's position at all times, the Coast Guard does not recommend that you use electronic charts for navigation. Their best use is for laying out a course before you go on a trip. Of the programs that are available, I recommend Nobeltek's Visual Navigation Suite, The Cap'n by Nautical Technologies, or Chart Viewer by Nautical Software. If you know your way around your local area and just want to check the tides, you can use a program called TideWare from Eldridge. This program uses information from the NOAA (National Oceanic and Atmospheric Administration) tide stations around the country to ensure that its predictions are accurate.

Marks

Vessel Lat/Lon:	41 08.530 N - 073 07.799 W	Start Time/Date:	07/01/1999 - 06:20:00	Vessel Speed Over Ground:		6.2 Kts
Name	**Lat**	**Lon**	**Rng To**	**Brg To**	**TTG**	**ETA**
001	41 08.537 N	073 07.879 W	0.060	277 T	00:00:35	06:20:35
002	41 12.935 N	072 05.134 W	47.371	084 T	07:38:25	13:58:26
003	41 15.205 N	071 50.937 W	58.218	083 T	09:23:24	15:43:24
004	41 18.396 N	071 27.786 W	75.867	082 T	12:14:11	18:34:12
005	41 27.808 N	071 22.058 W	81.741	076 T	13:11:02	19:31:02
006	41 29.065 N	071 20.583 W	83.107	075 T	13:24:15	19:44:16
007	41 28.783 N	071 19.531 W	83.807	075 T	13:31:01	19:51:02
008	41 29.088 N	071 19.563 W	83.855	075 T	13:31:29	19:51:30

Visual Navigation Suite™ - Copyright © 1995-1998 Nobeltec Corporation (800-495-6279) — Page 1

FIGURE 7.7 Each waypoint has a number; by inputting an average boat speed, the departure and arrival times can be estimated. This table shows the latitude and longitude of each waypoint, the distance to the next waypoint (Rng To), the bearing to the next waypoint (Brg To), the time to go (TTG), and the estimated time of arrival (ETA) for a trip planned for July 1, 1999.

Laying out your course with an electronic program is quite easy. You simply point your cursor where you are, click it, and then click on each turning point you will make. This is known as marking your waypoints. When you finish, you have a line that marks your entire course, known as your route. In the language of electronic navigation, this is known as planning a route or route planning. Save your route, and then click on the tide tables to see what the tide will be doing on the day you plan to be sailing. Just as with the paper chart, it helps to determine when the tide will be strongest either with or against you, so you can figure out where you want to be and at what time. By working backward from these positions, you can easily determine your starting time—but in this case the computer program does all the work for you.

Returning to the July 1, 1999, trip from Bridgeport to Newport, you can use the computer's tide program to find that the tide will be strongest in your favor at 14:00 hours (2 P.M.). Assuming an average speed of 6.2 knots, it will take seven hours and thirty-nine minutes to get to the Race from Bridgeport. This data is contained in the route-planning screen and is displayed in Figure 7.7. Simple calculations will tell you that your starting time should be around 6:20 A.M., and your arrival time in Newport should be about 20:00 hours or 8 P.M.

The advantage of laying a route out electronically is that you can take a portable computer aboard with a GPS to check visual bearings at any time. But if you choose to use an electronic navigation system, you should also keep a dead-reckoning position in the log and on a paper chart. This means you should check your position by buoys, lights, or features on shore as well. This way you have a backup should the batteries in your computer or GPS run low.

With your portable computer onboard, suppose you change your destination during the trip. You make it through the Race, but decide to go to Block Island instead. With two strokes of the mouse you change your destination. Now you'll steer 092 degrees and sail twelve nautical miles to reach Great Salt Pond on Block Island. (From there you can get a cab over to Ballards, one of the most famous restaurants in New England.) Be warned, though: The Coast Guard requires paper charts to be onboard even if you use a computer.

If you don't want to invest in a computer to bring aboard your boat, you can still use an electronic chart if you buy a plotter. This device takes the input from a GPS unit and uses an electronic chart to display a map on a very compact screen (often as small as two inches square). A GPS plotter automatically keeps track of where you are; you can also input waypoints and track your course, as well as any deviations from it.

GOING AGROUND USUALLY WON'T HURT YOU

Sailors used to think of the shore as a major nuisance. They would sooner be far out at sea. In fact, an old adage says, "It's not the sea that hurts you, it's the hard stuff around the edges." Suppose you do miss the buoy marking the entrance to a harbor and hit the bricks, as sailors say—what then? In most cases, going aground is nothing to worry about. Even the best captains put their vessel on the hard stuff once in a while. The skipper of the luxury liner *Queen Elizabeth II* managed to hit an uncharted rock while transiting Buzzards Bay Sound a few years ago.

Will going aground damage your boat? Possibly, but given the large lead keel hanging beneath it, you are more likely to put a dent in this keel than to actually harm the hull. On one memorable trip we missed the entrance to Florida's St. Augustine harbor in a thick fog and managed to put the boat on the sandy beach to the north of the channel. By using the engine, heeling the boat over, and rocking it, we got the boat off and made it back into the channel. The total damage was restricted to some paint removed from the bottom of the keel where we'd ground it into the sand. In the words of one of the crew, it gave a whole new meaning to sand-blasting!

On another trip we were following another boat into Hamilton Harbor in Bermuda. The boat was taking a shortcut and leaving the main channel. Our helmsman followed, thinking that if the boat ahead was flying a Bermudan flag, its crew must know where they were going. And indeed they did know the channel, but they also had a centerboard; we had a full keel. The thump we made when we hit a rock stopped the boat completely! After the craft was hauled to check for damage, we found that we had made a fist-sized gouge in the front of the keel about a foot above the bottom. That was the total extent of the damage—apart from a bruised ego on the part of the helmsman.

When you go aground, the first step is to find out what type of bottom you are on. Usually you can tell by the impact. A hard thunk usually means rocks or coral. A shuddering stop implies a pebble bottom. Coming to a gentle stop is a sign of a muddy bottom, though sand often gives the same type of response. How did I learn all this? At one time or another I have hit all these types of bottom.

How do you get the boat off once you have gone aground? First, try putting the engine astern. Usually you will have to heel the boat as well: Swing the boom out to one side and get all the crew on the same side. Some crews climb out onto the end of the boom, but you should only do this if you are wearing a life jacket and a harness attaching you to the boat. If going astern and heeling the boat fail, call on the radio and get somebody to haul you off.

When the boat comes to help you, make sure the towing hawser is fast to the primary winches (if they are towing from astern) and stand clear. If the hawser snaps, it can cause a serious injury. If your boat is to be towed clear from its bow, make the hawser fast around the mast, run it through the chocks, and stand clear. By all means heel the boat or run your own engine to help get off the mud.

Going aground in a protected area can subject you to large fines, up to thousands of dollars. In the Florida Keys there are large areas of fragile protected reefs; take particular care with your navigation. You also do not want to go aground in an area of heavy surf. You may never get your boat back onto open water.

CHAPTER 8

MIND YOUR MANNERS

On one cruise across the Atlantic Ocean a large tanker came into view about ten miles off our starboard bow. It was probably in the 150,000-ton range and was heading right at us. What do you do in these circumstances—get out of the way? Signal the ship? Or simply keep on sailing? We first located the ship on our radar and plotted its course. Then we called on the VHF radio. The skipper told us he had seen us on his own radar, and asked what we were. When we told him that we were a sailing vessel, he altered course and passed about a half mile to leeward of us. He had plenty of room in the middle of the ocean and willingly changed course to go around us. The men and women who operate these large ships are professional sailors; they don't want to run another vessel down. All it usually takes is a professional approach and normal courtesy.

An enclosed channel is a different matter. A large ship's passage is restricted by the depth of the channel, so don't expect it to avoid you; it's *your* responsibility to avoid the ship. This means that you should not cross in front of the ship; instead, go behind it. Large vessels take a long time to slow down. I once read that a 250,000-ton supertanker takes about ten miles to make an emergency stop after the engines are put in full reverse. Also, the bridge of many large ships is located well aft, so the people on the bridge cannot see a small sailing boat passing under the bow. And even if they do see a small sailboat approaching and disappearing in front of their bow, they'll have no idea whether they hit it, because of the size and inertia of their much larger vessel. Also, a large vessel is usually in a restricted channel and cannot maneuver to avoid you. This is why the responsibility to avoid a collision falls on you.

Of course, not all small-boat sailors recognize their responsibility. I live near the entrance to Narragansett Bay, and it's not unusual on a Sunday afternoon to hear five blasts of a large ship's horn as it tries to maneuver around Sunday sailors. If you hear five blasts on a ship's horn, it means that someone is in the way of the ship in a restricted channel. Check to see that you are not in the channel; if you are, head to one side quickly. If you cannot see the ship's bridge, the crew cannot see you. All the ship can do to avoid you is go astern, and that may not be enough. If the Coast Guard spots you or the vessel reports you, you can face a hefty fine, so keep clear of shipping in a channel.

RIGHT-OF-WAY RULES

When you take an afternoon drive down Main Street, you stay on your side of the yellow line and obey the laws of the road. In the same way sailors at sea have rules to enable them to avoid hitting each other. These rules are mandatory, but they are fairly simple and should be learned by heart and consistently obeyed. The first rule is that any action you take in a possible collision situation should be made in ample time, and should be aimed at avoiding the other vessel—whether you have the right-of-way or not. There is not much point arguing that you had right-of-way after you have sunk another boat.

You should also be cognizant of whether you are operating under inland rules or international rules—and know the differences. And pay attention to whether you are under sail or under power. In certain situations sailboats have different rights than they would if they were under power.

Just as there are rules for avoiding vessels under way, so are there rules for avoiding stationary vessels. All boats must avoid those that are at anchor or stopped. Of course, just as you are not allowed to park in the middle of Main Street, so boats must not anchor in a channel or a fairway where they may get hit by another vessel. Boats that are not under way must also display the appropriate lights and keep an anchor watch.

Rules of the road for boats under way are very similar to the rules of driving. For example, when you overtake another car, you first check to see that the road is clear and then you pass, keeping ample distance between you and the other vehicle. At sea, too, the rule is that the overtaking vessel keeps clear of the vessel being passed. When overtaking you should give the other boat plenty of room—at least one boat length. If two vessels pass close together, the Bernoulli effect can suck them together and cause them to collide. (The Bernoulli effect is the decrease in pressure that occurs as the velocity of a liquid is increased. In other words, when two vessels are moving on a parallel course, the velocity of the water moving between the vessels is increased and tends to suck the vessels together.)

In general, large vessels in traffic lanes have the right-of-way. The rule is specific in that it says, "A vessel under twenty meters (approximately sixty-six feet), sailing and fishing vessels shall not impede the passage of a vessel which can only navigate safely in a narrow channel or fairway." Smaller boats should also keep to the edge of the channel to allow larger vessels the right-of-way. There is even a ranking of responsibility to show who gives way to whom. If you are interested, you should obtain a copy of the *International Rules for Preventing Collisions at Sea*, known as COLREGS for short.

Because a vessel under power must give way to a vessel under sail, a powerboat must avoid a sailboat. However, if a sailboat has its engine running, it becomes a powerboat and must then avoid other sailboats.

When two closehauled sailboats are approaching each other, the one that has the wind on its starboard side has right-of-way. If both boats are sailing in approximately the same direction, the boat to windward must keep clear of the leeward boat. (See Figures

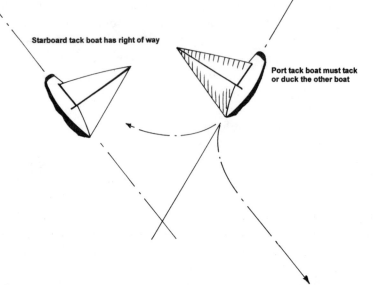

FIGURE 8.1A If two closehauled sailboats are converging, the boat that is on the starboard tack (has the wind over the starboard side) has the right-of-way. The port-tack boat must give way by either tacking onto starboard or by going astern of the other boat.

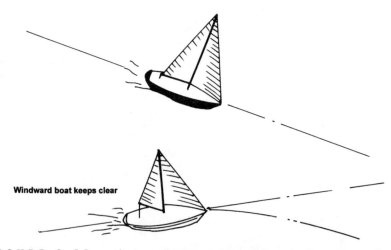

FIGURE 8.1B If two sailboats are converging, the boat that is close-hauled has the right-of-way. The boat that is to windward (the lower boat in this drawing) keeps clear. The boat sailing to windward loses a lot of ground if it has to bear off to avoid the other boat, so boats sailing to windward almost always have priority.

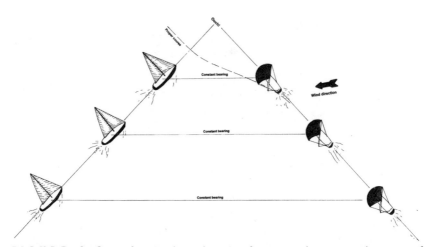

FIGURE 8.2 If you take a bearing from your boat onto the mast of another boat and the bearing does not change ("stays constant," sailors say), the two boats are on a collision course. In this scenario, the boat on the right gives way to the boat on the left, which is closehauled.

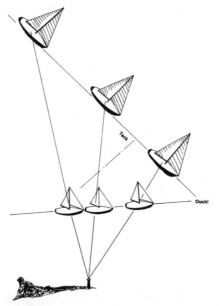

FIGURE 8.3 Another way to tell if you are on a collision course is to sight the land behind the boat you believe may hit you. If the boat's position relative to the land is constant, you will eventually hit. In this situation the lower boat is closehauled and has the right-of-way.

FIGURE 8.4   If two boats, under sail or power, are heading directly toward each other they should both turn to starboard to put their port sides toward the other boat. "Pass port to port or red to red," is the way sailors remember it.

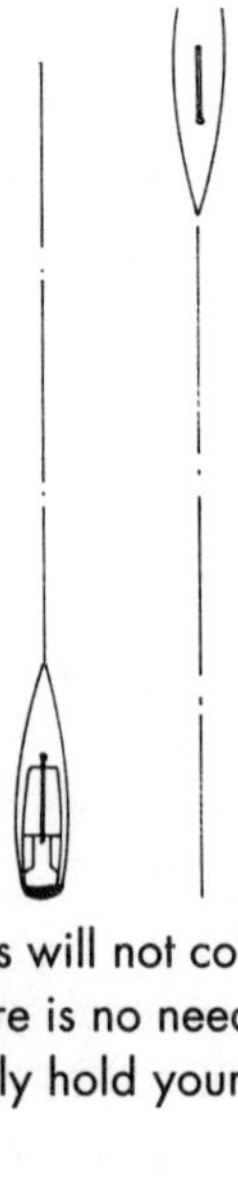

FIGURE 8.5   If two boats will not collide bow to bow, but will pass starboard side to starboard side, there is no need to cross the other boat's projected course to pass port to port. Simply hold your course and pass starboard to starboard.

8.1A and 8.1B. If you cannot tell on which side the wind is striking an approaching boat, keep clear.

You should always check whether you are on a collision course with another boat by taking a compass bearing on it. As Figure 8.2 shows, if the bearing does not change, you are on a collision course. Another way to check if you are on a collision course is to see whether the boat has land behind it. If it does and the land does not move relative to the other boat, you are on a collision course, as shown in Figure 8.3.

If two boats are closing head-on, they should both put their helms to port and pass port to port, unless they have agreed otherwise. This means the port bow of one vessel is opposite the port bow of the other, as shown in Figure 8.4. If one boat is to port of the other, there is no need to cross the other boat's track. Simply continue on course and cross starboard to starboard, as shown in Figure 8.5.

Similarly, if two powerboats are crossing at an angle, the boat with the other on its starboard side must keep clear and avoid crossing in front of the other boat. Note that a vessel restricted in its ability to to get out of the way—for example, a tug with a barge under tow—should be given the right-of-way. When you give another vessel the right-of-way, either hail it on the VHF radio or make an exaggerated turn to show that you are clearly yielding the right-of-way.

These are just a few of the collision regulations. The entire manual of regulations is the size of this book. You should obtain a current copy and learn the essential rules before venturing far offshore.

SIGNALS

Before the days of radar and large roaring engines, sailors used flags, sound signals, and night lights to tell other boats where they were going or where they were in poor visibility. When you are out sailing, you should listen and look for these signals. They tell you what is happening around you. For example, you may be sailing near a series of docks and hear three blasts of a horn. If you take no notice, you may be surprised to find a large ship backing out in front of you. Three blasts on a horn means that the ship is moving astern. In the inland rules of the road one prolonged blast means that a ship is leaving the dock, so it's important to know where the international rules give way to the inland rules.

Sound Signals

If two boats are meeting each other, they should signal their intent. In fact, many sound signals are mandatory when vessels are on a collision course unless VHF communication (channel 13) is used. If one boat intends to turn to starboard to avoid the other, the signal is one short blast. If a boat intends to turn to port, two short blasts must be sounded. Another sound signal you may hear is the five or more short blasts I mentioned earlier. If they are directed at you, they mean that you are in the way and should move immediately. Of course, sound signals are only used when in proximity to another vessel.

Nevertheless, they are especially important when operating in inland areas where high trees or buildings may obscure an approaching vessel. Once you have sounded a signal, make sure that you observe it. The skipper of the other boat will assume that you will obey it.

Fog Signals

Fog signals are a completely different matter. When fog rolls in or visibility is restricted, you should slow down and sound fog signals.

Listening for sounds or horns in fog is very difficult. Quite often I have found it hard to tell from which direction a horn is coming. If you have radar on your boat, you should turn it on in fog and detail someone to watch it all the time—someone who knows how to set the range and bearing, so you can track any vessels that might come near.

You should also proceed at a cautious speed in fog. According to admiralty courts, you should slow down to where you can stop in half of the available visibility. In other words, if visibility is two hundred yards, you should be able to stop in a hundred yards. While this might seem easy to do on a small boat, larger vessels may have trouble maintaining steerage if they travel at a speed that requires them to stop in a hundred yards, so they may be going faster than is prudent. It's also a wise precaution to turn on your navigation lights in fog. This will make it easier for other boats to see you.

Coast Guard regulations require that all vessels over twelve meters (39.2 feet) long carry a bell and a whistle or a foghorn. Foghorn signals are a mixture of short and long blasts. A long blast is four to six seconds, while a short blast is about one second. A gong or bell is sounded rapidly for five seconds.

A sailing boat under power or a powerboat should sound one long blast in fog at intervals of not more than two minutes. A boat under sail (as well as a fishing boat, and a boat restricted in its ability to maneuver) should make one long blast and two short ones every two minutes. This signal is also used by a sailboat that is not under way. A powerboat not under way or stopped sounds two long blasts, while a vessel being towed makes one long blast and three short ones.

When a boat of less than a hundred meters (less than 328 feet) is at anchor in fog, it should sound a bell at intervals of less than one minute. If the boat is more than a hundred meters long, it may sound a gong as well. Any boat at anchor in fog can also sound a short, long, short series of blasts on its horn. This, it's hoped, will prevent a collision between an anchored vessel and a boat under way. Boats of less than twelve meters need not make these signals, but must make some noise at least every two minutes.

WHAT IS THAT?

Sailing at night can be very relaxing. You gaze at the heavens, watch the moon make its way across the sky, occasionally see a meteor as it burns up in the atmosphere, and enjoy the sight of other vessels far off in the darkened sea. Typically, because of your eye level on a sailboat, you might only be able to see other vessels five to ten miles away. If you climbed to the masthead, you might see vessels twenty miles away.

But night lights can be confusing when viewed against the background of lights on shore. One trick is to look for lights that are moving against the background of fixed lights. Another is to look out of the side of your eye at the lights. Quite often you will first pick up the light when you are not looking directly at it.

When you see a buoy at night, make sure you time its flash carefully. We once thought we'd have to go around a red light that our navigator was sure was displaying four flashes every minute. It turned out that the buoy with that particular characteristic was another three miles on. The light we saw displayed *six* flashes every minute and was actually a lighthouse half a mile inshore. We would have had great difficulty going around it.

When you see a car or truck parked by the side of a road, it is clearly stopped and may have its hazard lights on. Often it's hard to tell if a boat is stopped or anchored, however, or whether the skipper is just making a cup of coffee while the boat continues on its way under autopilot. For this reason, there are certain signals that tell an approaching boat what another boat is doing.

Some of these signals identify types of vessels in addition to their current operations. For example, a police, Coast Guard, or enforcement vessel has a blue flashing light that is turned on for emergencies. These lights are shown in addition to the normal navigation lights when the vessel is under way at night. A submarine displays a yellow flashing light that flashes three times per second for three seconds followed by a three-second period with no light. A fireboat or rescue boat may display flashing red lights as it speeds toward the scene of a fire or accident.

All vessels are required to carry navigation lights, but they differ depending on the size and job of the vessel. Navigation lights are red, green, and white. White lights are almost always on the centerline of the ship and are either masthead, range, or stern lights. Red lights are on the port side of the vessel, green lights on the starboard side of the vessel. Remember that *port* and *starboard* refer to the left and right sides of a boat, respectively, when you are standing on the boat facing the bow. When another boat is coming toward you, port and starboard will be reversed.

A sailboat coming directly toward you will have a red and green bow light visible, as shown in Figure 8.6, but no masthead light. If that boat puts the engine on, it becomes a powerboat and must display a white light, just like the powerboat in Figure 8.7. Any ship of less than fifty meters (164 feet) must display a single white masthead light. Ships of more than fifty meters (164 feet)

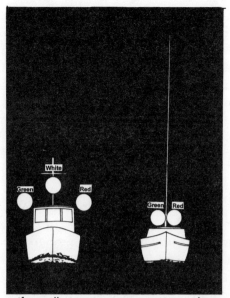

FIGURE 8.6   If a sailboat turns on its engine, it becomes a powerboat and must show a white masthead light, sometimes called a steaming light. Powerboats less than fifty meters (164 feet) in length also show this arrangement of lights (right).

FIGURE 8.7   A sailboat under sail headed directly toward you at night will often show only a red and green light. It may also show a tricolor masthead light or a red over green masthead light (left).

must display a second light on an after mast higher than the first light. These are the basic lights that all vessels should display. For some vessels of less than seven meters, it may not be possible to carry the mandatory navigation lights. In this case, it is acceptable to show an all-around white light, or to use an electric flashlight. Very small boats such as dinghies can also use a flashlight.

Each navigation light is a special style and has a particular range of view. Each sidelight must cover an arc of 112.5 degrees (ten points on the compass). The masthead light covers an arc of 225 degrees (twenty points), and the stern light covers an arc of 135 degrees (twelve points). Range lights (those carried on an after and higher mast than the normal navigation lights) cover an arc of 225 degrees (twenty points). These arcs are shown in Figure 8.8.

Knowing the arcs that these lights cover can help you determine whether a vessel is crossing your boat or on a collision course with it. For example, if you can see a red and green bow light with a white masthead light just above them, you know that you are dead ahead of a boat that's less than fifty meters long.

Not only should you learn to read navigation lights, but you should also understand other lights if you intend to sail at night. If at any time you see a red and a green light, with a white light in the middle of them, look out—you are directly in front of a large ship! If the red light then disappears, leaving the green light and white masthead light visible, the boat has turned and is moving at a slightly different angle to you. If the white masthead light disappears, the boat is clearly crossing. Shortly, you can expect the green light to disappear also, and the white stern light to appear.

If you see a red light (red means danger), the vessel showing the red light has the right-of-way, as long as both boats are under power. A sailboat has the right-of-way over a powerboat as long as the powerboat is under normal control (isn't fishing, for example) and is not restricted by draft. Other lights that you might see are on a pilot boat (white over red), a fishing boat either under way or at anchor (red over white), a fishing boat that is towing a trawl

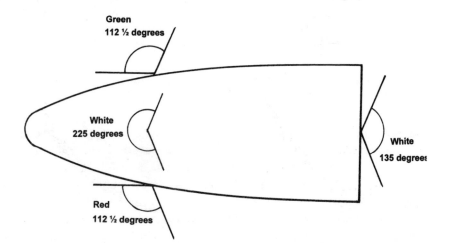

FIGURE 8.8 Each light must shine over specific angles. Each sidelight (red and green) covers an angle of 112.5 degrees from the centerline. Masthead and range lights cover an arc of 225 degrees (112.5 degrees on either side of the center line). The stern light covers an arc of 135 degrees. In this manner a light is showing no matter what angle a boat is viewed from.

(green over white), and a boat that is not under command—say, a lobster boat that has no one at the helm while the skipper is tending pots (two red lights on the mast).

As I mentioned earlier, sailboats carry normal navigation lights, but under sail a sailboat does not carry a white masthead light. However, when the engine is turned on, the sailboat becomes a powerboat and should carry an all-around white light on the mast. A sailboat less than twenty meters (sixty-six feet) long can also carry a masthead light divided into red, green, and white segments, as shown in Figure 8.9A. This light is optional and may be carried as well as the normal lights. Another light for larger sailboats is the red over green all-around light at or near the masthead, as shown in Figure 8.9B.

If you approach an anchored vessel, you might notice a black ball hanging from the yard or from a mast in the forward part of the ship, as shown in Figure 8.10. This is displayed in daytime to show that the ship is anchored. Note that navigation lights are not

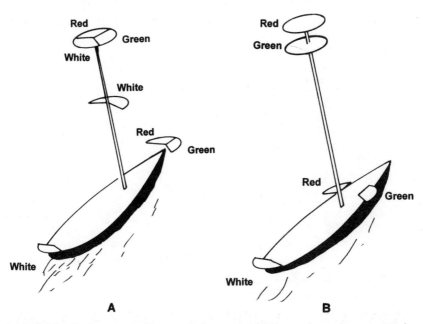

FIGURE 8.9 A sailboat with the optional lights is shown here. In (A) the boat has a tricolor masthead light, and in (B) the boat is showing a red over green all-around light. These lights are shown in addition to normal navigation lights.

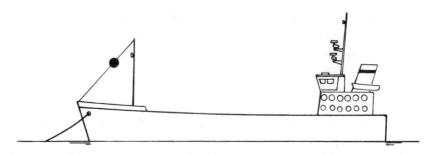

FIGURE 8.10 A black ball hanging in the forward part of any vessel shows that the vessel is anchored. At night the black ball is replaced by an all-around white light.

shown when the vessel is anchored at night; then, the black ball is replaced by an all-around white light in the forward part of the boat. And there are some areas, known as special anchorages (near

Day

FIGURE 8.11A A fishing vessel that is not moving may have the entire crew working on the nets. It may also move unexpectedly, so keep clear. The signal to show that the boat is not under command is a black ball in the forepart of the boat if it's less than twenty meters (sixty-six feet). Fishing vessels longer than this should show a pair of cones with the top one inverted.

a yacht club or marina), where vessels can anchor without showing lights. Also, vessels of less than seven meters (twenty-two feet) need not show an anchor light as long as they are out of normal navigation channels. Vessels of more than a hundred meters (328 feet) must show normal deck lights when at anchor.

Fishing vessels should show two cones in a vertical line in the forward part of the boat, but a fishing boat of less than twenty meters may display a basket in the forward part of the boat, as shown in Figure 8.11A. Note that the fishing boat would usually display navigation lights if it were stopped at sea, as shown in Figure 8.11B, but it would not display navigation lights if it were at anchor. It's always wise to keep away from fishing vessels; they may have gear deployed, or they may suddenly start up and turn in an unexpected direction.

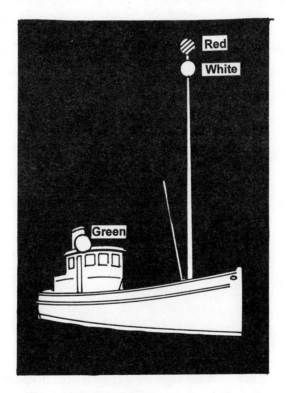

Night

FIGURE 8.11B   At night a fishing vessel shows a red over white masthead light in addition to normal navigation lights.

This brief summary is by no means comprehensive. It is intended to give you an idea of the more commonly used rules and signals. Many good books are available on these subjects, and you should keep one onboard your boat. You never know when you'll need it.

DISTRESS CALLS AND SIGNALS

There are a number of visual signals that should be shown if you get into trouble. Unfortunately, many of them seem to be ignored, or few boaters take the time to learn and observe them. I bet that if you were to display an orange flag with a black ball and square in the center, only a few boaters would actually come to your aid. If you were to display code flags *N* and *C* (November and Charlie), almost nobody would rush to help you. Both are emergency signals.

A fire in a bucket is also an emergency signal, but you are more likely to burn your boat down with one than to get the assistance you seek. Burning your boat, however, *will* get attention!

These days you are far more likely to get a response when you yell "Mayday" on channel 16, or light off your EPIRB (Emergency Position Indicating Response Beacon). But this is not to say you shouldn't keep a lookout for emergency signals of any kind. Still, be aware of what signals work best in any given situation. Flares, whether red or white, parachute or meteor, are far more likely to get a response during the hours of darkness than an orange flag with a black square and a ball. A foghorn sounded continuously or people waving their arms will elicit more responses than a yellow dye marker in the water. And smoke always attracts a response.

It's also said that most sailors would recognize an American flag flown upside down as a distress signal. I once saw such a flag, and the comment from the mostly American crew was, "Silly fool, hoisted his flag upside down." When the person onboard then waved the flag on its staff, we investigated to find that the single-handed sailor had scalded himself and needed help.

Any signal can mean that a boat needs help, and as a sailor you should always investigate unless you feel it's a hoax or a trap. Out at sea you should also sail courteously near another boat, if only to pass a bit of conversation. One boat we passed in midocean asked to be reported to its yacht club, because its single-side-band (long-range) radio had gotten wet and was not working. We communicated with this boat by VHF radio, which has a range of line of sight (about ten to twenty miles) and was not powerful enough to reach the shore. In the middle of a sailing crisis you will be glad you know the proper procedures.

CHAPTER 9

SAFETY

S ailing, like any other sport, can be dangerous. Being prepared helps minimize the dangers and lets you get on with enjoying the sail. In fact, I often find that the more prepared I am, the less likely I am to need to need assistance.

WHAT TO WEAR

Safety starts with having the right clothes onboard. If you go out on the water in spring, you will find that it's much colder than being on land. Without some warm clothes you may get mild hypothermia, which will most definitely reduce your enjoyment of the sail. You don't need a whole new wardrobe to go sailing, but a few tips on what to wear will be useful. At the top of your list of things to consider should probably be shoes.

Shoes

You don't need boat shoes to go sailing, although you do need footwear of the nonskid variety. When I first went sailing, I wore sneakers, and they served perfectly well. Another time I accidentally took my gardening boots instead of my sailing boots. Although they left big muddy footprints, they certainly kept the water out! On many boats I have sailed barefoot, but you need to be very familiar with the boat before you try this technique. It's easy to stub your toe on a cleat or deck block, and that really hurts.

Before you invest in boat shoes, you should learn a little about them. Manufacturers make these shoes with two types of bottoms, one for street use and the other for onboard use. Onboard shoes have a softer sole than street shoes, but this sole is more slip resistant. If you wear onboard shoes on the street, their softer sole will wear out fairly quickly. I found that wearing the softer-bottomed shoe in the street shortened its life to about three to four months. Street shoes have a harder bottom, usually colored a light brown and called Vibram. These last a lot longer but are not the best for onboard wear. I find that I get about eight to ten months' wear from a street shoe.

The uppers of boat shoes are made of leather for water resistance. In my experience the stitching is the first part of the shoe to break; I have a needle and palm and can resew broken stitching. I don't polish the uppers like many people do. Polish preserves them, but in my opinion it looks odd. I do, however, treat the uppers with one of the oils designed for the job.

In my closet I have boat shoes from Sebago, Topsider, and L.L. Bean. Two pairs have white stains from dried salt water. No matter how much the shoe is washed, this stain doesn't come out. All the shoes have a reasonable life span and cost about seventy-five to ninety-five dollars. Another pair are Chinese-made shoes that cost $29.95 and lasted until the check cleared the bank. I sent them back to the manufacturer when they split along the leather seam. Since then I have resewn the seam twice, but the leather tears fairly quickly. Of all of my boat shoes, L.L. Bean's have lasted the longest.

When you first go sailing on someone else's boat, ask what shoes to bring along. Some owners don't like street shoes worn onboard, while others don't seem to mind. If an owner objects strongly to street shoes, carry your boat shoes and put them on when you step aboard.

For deep-water cruising or sailing in heavy weather, you should have a pair of sailing boots. They are available from most major boating outlets or chandleries. The cost of a typical pair of sailing boots can range from $40 to $180. When purchasing a pair, check their nonskid properties. You are unlikely to wear them on the street, so durability of the sole is not a major concern.

Foul-Weather Gear

When you are out sailing in rainy weather, there is nothing quite so nice as having dry clothes under your foul-weather gear. But how do you know before you go sailing that your foul-weather gear will keep the rain out? The simplest test is to wear it in a shower for ten minutes. Then take it off and inspect the inside carefully. If it shows signs of wetness, imagine what it will be like after three and a half hours standing watch in cold, rainy weather!

I have tried many types of foul-weather gear and strongly recommend Henri-Lloyd of England. This company once made the very best gear, but other manufacturers have gained considerable ground over the last few years. Musto, Helly Hanson, and Douglas Gill now make excellent gear as well.

The type of gear you select should be based on the type of sailing that you do. If you'll be offshore, buy the best quality you can afford. You may spend a lot of time in wet weather without a lot of time to dry off. The shorter the length of time you spend sailing, the less expensive your foul-weather gear can be. Many dinghy sailors, for example, use a one-piece suit with elastic cuffs at the neck, ankles, and wrists. Even if they go for a swim, they will get ashore within an hour or so.

On spring days when the sun is shining it might seem warm on shore, but the water is often much colder, and the wind seems to cut right through a sweater. For this reason, you should carry a lightweight, windproof jacket to wear over your sweater. It will keep you much warmer. Picking the right gear for the occasion is something that you will learn. A good rule of thumb when you first go sailing is to ask what you should wear and always bring an extra sweater.

Staying Warm

If you want to make yourself really miserable, go sailing early in the season without enough warm clothes. You'll get cold quickly, and you'll stay cold. Believe me, I've been there. You'd think that at the end of June, the weather in New England would be reasonably warm, wouldn't you? I thought so, too, the first time I raced to Bermuda.

The first night of the race was cold, with a temperature only just above freezing. "Brass monkey weather," sailors sometimes call it. In the days of sailing ships the tray holding cannonballs that sat next to a gun was called a monkey. The cannonballs were made of cast iron, and for ceremonial use the tray was made of brass. In very cold weather the cannonballs would shrink and slide off the brass monkey, giving rise to the adage, "Weather cold enough to freeze the balls off a brass monkey." I had expected a warm evening and was very cold until I got off watch. Since that time I have always taken plenty of warm clothing, even on a cruise in Florida.

Clothing is warmest in layers. A T-shirt topped by a sailing shirt and a sweater can easily be supplemented with a fleece pullover or a thermal jacket. If you get too warm, you can simply discard the outermost layer. A lightweight, windproof jacket is also important. A sailboat won't sail without wind, but that same wind can cut through sweaters like a knife through butter. If you need a heavier jacket, use your foul-weather gear. Make sure you take one or two pairs of socks along, even if you don't normally wear them. Wind, even a moderately warm breeze, hitting bare skin can make you feel cold fairly quickly. And always bring extra warm clothing if there is any chance of rain. The only thing worse than being cold is being cold and wet.

When you pack clothes for a long trip, you might want to put complete changes of clothes into plastic bags fastened with a twist-tie or a zipper top. This will ensure that clothes stay dry even if your bag gets soaked. During one boat delivery from Southampton, England, to Bremerhaven, Germany, we hit a force eight gale—gusting to force ten—in the English Channel. The boat had relatively shallow bilges, and water got everywhere. Everything was soaked apart from the changes of clothing I had packed in plastic bags. After the gale had blown out, it was a real relief to change into dry clothes.

Hats

The possibility of skin cancer has recently encouraged more and more sailors to use sunblock and wear hats or visors. If you use a hat at sea (and you should), pick one with a wide-enough brim to protect your eyes and face. A baseball-type cap or the floppy white "Tilley" hat often sold at boat shows will work fine. For heavier weather a sou'wester-style hat is by far the best. (It looks rather like a soft, rubberized version of a fireman's helmet.) This hat will keep water out of your face, letting it run off outside your collar. Any hat should be secured with a strap of some kind. You'll be surprised how many times your hat will blow off while you are on the water.

Sunglasses

For sun protection you should also wear sunglasses. I use the darkest polarized glasses I can find. Glare and reflections off the water can nearly double the damage done to your eyes compared to what you would encounter the same day ashore. You should also make sure that your sunglasses are attached with a string or line so they will not fall overboard.

Sunscreen

Yes, you do need sunscreen. You should apply one with an SPF (sun protection factor) of at least 15 before going out on a boat. It should be reapplied every few hours if the weather is wet or if you sweat a lot.

WHAT DO YOU NEED TO BE SAFE?

What should you have onboard your boat in case of an emergency? Life jackets are mandated by the Coast Guard, as are foghorns, fire extinguishers, and flares. The ORC (Offshore Racing Council) also requires harnesses, bilge pumps, life rafts, and various other items of equipment for sailing boats that compete in races under ORC regulations. But most cruising boats lack a good inventory of equipment to cover the entire spectrum of safety at sea. Here are some things that should be aboard every boat that ventures more than five miles away from land.

A First-Aid Kit

Every boat should carry a first-aid kit. The type of kit you carry, however, will depend on the type of sailing you are doing. If you only sail afternoons or weekends, an inshore-level kit is fine. If you sail for two weeks while on vacation away from home, this same kit will probably serve your purpose. However, you should also include prescription medicines (you may have to get a special prescription from your doctor) and any other unusual medical items that would be hard to substitute at sea.

First-aid kits come in all shapes and sizes, with different types and amounts of equipment. The smaller kits are intended only for minor problems such as cuts, stings, splinters, sunburn, mild abrasions, and other conditions that you would typically treat at home with a medicated cream and a Band-Aid. Typically, the smaller kits come with a booklet explaining how to perform minor first aid.

In addition to your standard first-aid kit, another small kit should be assembled with items to treat common ailments such as colds, stomachaches, and diarrhea. When you think about what to put in this kit, look at the items you have in your medicine cabinet at home.

As you travel farther offshore and farther away from assistance, your medical kit should become more comprehensive. Upgrade your first-aid skills as well by taking first-aid, CPR, and other emergency courses. This type of training can be obtained through the Red Cross. Your local doctor or hospital might also know where training courses are held.

The first-aid books you carry onboard should also be more advanced when you plan an ocean passage. Remember, on an ocean crossing you may be away from land for two or three weeks. You cannot visit an emergency room or call an ambulance to help you. When at sea the nearest help is usually the Coast Guard, and because they have to come by boat, they may take a while. If you are far at sea, the Coast Guard usually arrives by helicopter or directs a nearby ship to your aid, and this may take several hours. In the event of an emergency, first aid must be applied by the people onboard, which means that they need good medical equipment and information.

It helps to get a checkup before you leave to minimize the chances of medical problems cropping up. The checkup should include a dental and eyeglass check, too. You don't want to be several hundred miles at sea and get a toothache or drop your only pair of prescription glasses in the ocean. There are dental kits available for sailors, and a second pair of eyeglasses is always helpful.

In the Bermuda race back in the 1970s, the fleet doctor took his duties a little too seriously: Boats were required to carry clamps, hemostats, and other exotic equipment that could only be obtained from a licensed physician. We jumped through hoops to get all the gear, even though no crew member had any idea how to use it. Today you can buy preassembled medical kits that contain virtually all the equipment you would need for a prolonged ocean crossing. If you cannot obtain a medical kit or have any medical questions relating to sailing, you should talk to your physician.

WHERE TO FIND FIRST-AID KITS FOR BOATS
Medical Sea Pak Company
1945 Ridge Road East
Rochester, NY 14622
Tel: (800) 832-6954

Life-Assist, Inc.
11355-B Pyrites Way, #16
Rancho Cordova, CA 95670
Tel: (800) 824-6016

General Scientific Safety Equipment Company
525 Spring Garden Street
Philadelphia, PA 19123-2899
Tel: (800) 523-0166

A dental kit containing a dental emergency manual, temporary filling material, Eugenol, and Orabase with benzocaine is available from:

DentiMedic
102 Eighth Street
Pocomoke City, MD 21851
Tel: (410) 957-0788

WHAT YOU SHOULD HAVE IN A FIRST-AID KIT   The entire kit should be in a plastic (Tupperware-style) waterproof container. The kits developed by Medical Sea Pak include all the items listed below.

For sailing within ten to twenty miles of shore:

Adhesive strips (Band-Aids)
Sterile cotton wadding
Gauze bandages
Elastic bandages
Eye pads
Adhesive tape
Zinc oxide ointment
Motion sickness tablets
Sterile wound wipes
Aspirin or nonaspirin pain reliever
Tweezers
Scissors
Sunscreen (at least SPF 15)
Sunburn cream
Fishhook remover kit

Seasickness

Many people get seasick. Even Admiral Lord Nelson, one of the most famous sailors of all time, got seasick. It decreases your enjoyment of sailing and can be a safety risk if you are so sick as to be disabled. Quite often the easiest way not to become seasick is to spend the night aboard the boat before you set sail. If that doesn't work, there are many remedies, which range from a ginger-based soft drink called Smooth Sailing to pills, wristbands with buttons, and a scopalamine patch (Transderm Scop) that is placed behind your ear. Before you commit to spending a large amount of time at

For offshore sailing:

All of the items above, plus:
2" and 4" gauze bandages
2" and 4" elastic bandages
Abdominal pads
Gauze pads
Iodine wipers
Cold pack
Triangular bandages
Butterfly closures
Eye irrigation kit
Ammonia inhalants
Extra rolls of adhesive tape
First-aid booklet
Rescue blanket
Rubber gloves
Inflatable splint
Scalpel or very sharp knife
Burn and scald relief kit
Antibiotic ointment

You should also include prescription medicines and any other items suggested by your doctor.

sea, find out if you are prone to seasickness and try different remedies to see which one is best for you.

Life Jackets

Life jackets are mandatory onboard all boats, although wearing them is not. However, they may be of different styles, depending on where the boat will travel. The highest-quality life jacket is the Type I PFD (personal flotation device)—the most buoyant and effective jacket, according to the Coast Guard. It is designed to turn an unconscious person face-up and has a minimum of twenty-two pounds of buoyancy to support an adult in open, rough water. A Type II PFD serves the same functions as a Type I but has only 15.5 pounds of buoyancy. This type is best suited for calm inland waters or where rescue patrols are nearby. A Type III PFD also has 15.5 lbs of buoyancy, but is designed to keep a conscious person vertical or slightly backward in calm waters. Type III PFDs have three specialized subgroups: flotation aids, waterski vests (for waterskiing enthusiasts), and float coats (a coat that has built-in buoyancy). Each meets the Coast Guard definition of a Type III, but each serves a slightly different purpose. Type IV PFDs are throwable devices such as cushions, horseshoes, or life rings. They have at least 16.5 pounds of buoyancy and are intended to be thrown to a person in the water. Type V PFDs are special-use units such as white-water rafting vests.

The Coast Guard requires that there be enough PFDs onboard for every crew member, and there must be at least one Type IV throwable device. ORC regulations for offshore boats require two throwable devices, such as horseshoes with poles and drogues (devices used to slow the boat).

Recently, U.S. Sailing made it mandatory for sailors to wear life jackets when starting and finishing a race under its aegis. The Coast Guard is about to approve inflatable PFDs, and is collecting data about mandatory use. It appears, then, that the trend is toward greater and greater use of PFDs.

Life Rafts

In France and some other European countries life rafts are mandatory, but the U.S. Coast Guard does not require that every recreational boat have one. For sailboats racing offshore, the ORC mandates a life raft with enough space to hold every person in the crew. The best life rafts are totally self-inflating, with two or more buoyancy compartments, a canopy to protect the occupants against the elements, a package of safety equipment, and all the requirements needed to conform to SOLAS (International Convention for the Safety of Life at Sea).

By keeping the occupants out of the water, a life raft helps prevent hypothermia. It gathers the crew together so that the group's heat can be used to keep everyone warm. It also makes a much larger and easier object to spot than the heads of people floating in the water. A properly packed life raft and a grab bag offer far more life support than simply swimming in the water can. A life raft with a canopy will also help prevent severe sunburn or exposure. You should only board a life raft, however, if your boat is in immediate danger of sinking. The old adage that you should "step up to your life raft" makes a good operating credo.

In a demonstration at a Zodiac life raft factory, I saw a life raft inflate in less than forty-five seconds, plenty of time to allow the crew to get off a sinking vessel. According to the experts at Zodiac, packing a life raft in a plastic canister is a more secure method of carrying it. The canister protects the raft against UV degradation, keeps it waterproof, and can be stepped on without damaging the raft. If you invest in a life raft, you should also put together a grab bag of essential items that may not be in the raft itself. And note that according to the folks at Zodiac (who study every usage of a life raft), the first thing that happens when people board one is that they get seasick.

Fire Extinguishers

Another item that the Coast Guard requires on all boats is a fire extinguisher. Boats of less than twenty-six feet must carry one B-I Coast Guard–approved fire extinguisher. Boats of from twenty-six to forty feet must carry a minimum of two B-I USCG-approved extinguishers or one B-II type, while boats of from forty to sixty-five feet must carry three B-I types or one B-I and one B-II type. Boats of more than sixty-five feet must meet federal standards. The difference between the two main types of extinguisher has to do with their capacities. A B-I extinguisher carries at least 1.25 gallons of foam, 2 pounds of dry chemical, or 2.5 pounds of Halon or its equivalent (because of its ozone-depleting qualities, Halon is no longer manufactured, and alternatives are being used), or 4 pounds of CO_2. A B-II type extinguisher has a greater fire-fighting capacity.

Obviously, you should purchase the type of extinguisher that will fight the type of fire you are most likely to encounter. Chemical extinguishers are best on fuel or grease fires, so you would probably want to have one near the galley and the engine compartment. CO_2 extinguishers are best on fires that are contained in a closed space and fueled by wood or other solid materials. Apart from the engine compartment and cabins, there are few completely enclosed spaces on most boats, so a CO_2 extinguisher may not work well in many locations.

I recommend that one fire extinguisher be located in the forward part of the boat, one in or near the galley, one in or near the engine compartment, and—if your boat has an aft cabin—one there as well. You cannot have too many fire extinguishers located in strategic areas around your boat.

Harnesses

Harnesses are essential on sailboats, especially if somebody has to go to the top of the mast. There are no Coast Guard specifications for harnesses, but since the Fastnet disaster in 1979, the ORC has imposed stringent harness criteria. (In 1979 the 235-boat Fastnet race fleet was hit by a major storm with wind speeds of fifty-five knots, gusting to seventy knots. Twenty-four boats were abandoned and fifteen people died.)

The webbing on all harnesses should be strongly sewn (in many cases it's double- or triple-sewn). All harnesses should have a breaking strength of more than 1,500 kilograms (thirty-three hundred pounds), and the harness tether must have a breaking strength of more than 2,080 kilograms (about forty-six hundred pounds). This is because ORC tests showed that a tether often broke long before the harness gave way. (This standard has been under careful investigation since the Sydney-Hobart disaster in December 1998.) Tethers should not be more than two meters (about six feet) long, to prevent injury if a crew member loses balance and is held by the harness. Tethers should also have an extra hook so that one hook is attached at all times. There should never be an occasion when a crew member is on the deck without a lifeline that's attached by one hook. Hooks on the end of the harness should be inspected to make sure they cannot come undone accidentally.

Distress Flares

Flares that meet the SOLAS regulations are designed for use aboard all commercial shipping around the world. Similar flares are used on recreational vessels worldwide. (Flares are also packed in life rafts, which may be shipped worldwide.) Flares are required by the U.S. Coast Guard. A more comprehensive flare kit is required aboard ocean-racing sailboats that race under ORC regulations. These regulations are pretty good standards for all boats, be they sail or power. The ORC recommends that boats that sail close to shore ("category 4 racers," in ORC terminology) carry a minimum of four red hand flares and four white hand flares. Boats that sail offshore (category 1) are required to carry a minimum of twelve white parachute flares, four red hand flares, four white hand flares, and two orange smoke signals. Boats that sail in the in-between categories (2 and 3) must carry four red hand flares, four white hand flares, four parachute flares, and two smoke signals.

All flares should be checked yearly and discarded if they have passed their expiration date. When setting off handheld flares, hold them over the side of your boat. The hot slag that drips from them can burn your boat.

Distress Flags and Mirrors

In my opinion, distress flags and mirrors are unlikely to be taken seriously by the average boater unless the vessel in distress is the only one in sight. Unfortunately, boaters flying an orange distress flag with a black circle and square are often just as likely to be asked what country the flag is from as they are to get rescued. A reflecting mirror is useful if you are in a life raft, but reflections abound on the ocean, and if you are on a boat with a broken engine or a boat that is sinking slowly, flares will bring assistance faster than the reflection from a mirror. Of course, if your supply of flares has run out or you have nothing else, distress flags and mirrors may be the only signals you have left.

Radar Reflectors

Radar reflectors are essential if you plan to sail in foggy areas, but not all such reflectors give off an equally strong signal. When purchasing a radar reflector, there are a number of features to look for; the most important is the return signal strength. However, do not rely on your radar reflector's ability too strongly. I was once aboard a yacht in thick fog that had a twenty-inch intersecting-plane reflector flying, and we were almost run down by a freighter. When we contacted the freighter, they told us that they could not see our radar echo against the clutter, even though we were flying a reflector.

The best reflector may be the Cyclops-3 passive radar reflector, which has been found to exceed ISO (International Standards Organization) 8729: 1987 specifications, as well as IMO (International Maritime Organization) specs. It is also accepted by insurance companies. The reflector design is based on dielectric lens technology, which focuses the incoming signal to reflect back a stronger signal. There are three models for different sizes of boats. Another top-notch reflector is the Lensref from Varigas International in Timonium, Maryland. This one uses a Luneberg lens to concentrate the signal and reflect it back to the ship using radar. Reports from seaborne use indicate that both of these radars make a boat visible on radar screens at ranges of up to fifteen miles. Both reflectors are virtually unstowable, being quite large; they're best permanently mounted on the masthead, but not attached to the front or rear of the mast, where the mast can block the radar signal.

If you do not plan to have your radar reflector permanently fixed to your mast or to the highest point on your boat, it should be stowed. The intersecting-plane reflectors that can be taken apart and stowed under a bunk are very popular. The size of these reflectors is proportional to the return signal strength. However, tests indicate that these reflectors actually work about 25 percent of the time. With the trend toward automatic watch keeping on large ships, fewer crew are actually looking at the ocean; radar is being used as a collision avoidance device. Typically, a blip has to show on three revolutions of the radar to trip an alarm. If your reflector is working only 25 percent of the time, it will not often trip a radar alarm unless you are lucky. The effectiveness of a radar reflector is also directly related to its height: The higher it is, the better the return.

EPIRBs

If you decide to sail offshore, the most important safety item you should buy is an EPIRB (Emergency Position Indicating Radio Beacon). These are satellite beacons: A radio signal is transmitted to a satellite, which alerts a ground station to the whereabouts of the EPIRB. Because the rescue operation homes in on the EPIRB signal after a satellite has found it, you should not turn your EPIRB on and off. Leave it on.

There are two types of EPIRBs available, the 121.5 MHz and the 406 MHz. The 121.5-frequency EPIRBs are less expensive than the 406 models by a factor of about four, but these lower-frequency models suffer more problems as well. For one thing, they set off a lot of false alarms. According to some experts, the rate of false alarms for a 406 EPIRB is about eight to ten per real rescue, while a 121.5 MHz EPIRB has about a thousand false alarms per real rescue. Be careful that you do not set off any false alarms. You can be charged for the cost of the rescue services. Typically, these costs are in the range of four to five thousand dollars per hour per aircraft.

Another problem with lower-frequency EPIRB models is that they may not be "heard" by aircraft in areas of radio clutter. This means that a person with a 406 EPIRB is usually rescued long before a person with a 121.5 EPIRB. You are probably much better off spending more money and sailing secure in the knowledge that your EPIRB will be heard if it goes off.

EPIRBs on the 406 MHz frequency are specifically designed to work with SARSATs (search and rescue satellites), but they need to be registered. The registration gives the owner's name, address, and type of vessel—information that is invaluable to any rescuer.

The latest type of EPIRB has a built-in GPS (Global Positioning System) and is known as a GPIRB*. This not only transmits an emergency signal but gives the location of the EPIRB as well.

KEEPING IN TOUCH WITH SATELLITE COMMUNICATIONS

With more and more satellites going aloft, it is now possible to keep in touch from anywhere in the world. In fact, in most areas you don't even need a satellite. Many cell phones work up to twenty miles at sea. But if you go beyond coastal areas, satellite communications are your link back home. We used Inmarsat—a satellite-based telephone system used by shipping worldwide—when we were in the middle of the Atlantic, although this takes a

---

* GPIRB is a registered trademark of Northern Airborne Technology.

large antenna and is expensive. There are a number of systems, with more becoming available.

HYPOTHERMIA

There are times when even with the best safety equipment, you may end up in the water. If you do, you are likely to face one of the greatest dangers related to sailing: hypothermia. Hypothermia is what happens when you get cold beyond your external body parts (fingers and toes) and into the core of your body—your heart and lungs. It can happen not just if you fall into cold water, but also if you sit on your boat in cold weather for too long without adequate protection.

When you are out sailing in the spring and fall, make sure you stay warm and dry. Adequate layers of clothing such as mittens or gloves, a scarf, a warm hat, a life jacket, and warm boots are all essential to staying warm. It's a lot easier to stay warm than it is to get warm. If you feel that you are getting cold, get below, where you are out of the wind and where you can stay warm. If the weather is going to be particularly cold, or you are going to be in the water, you should also consider a wet or dry suit.

If the worst happens and you fall over the side into cold water, you have a limited amount of time to get out. In cold water you lose body heat twenty-five to fifty times faster than in air. A life jacket can help you survive cold water in two ways. It provides insulation that keeps you warmer, and it keeps you afloat so that you do not have to expend energy trying to tread water. You should huddle into a heat-conserving position (knees up and arms wrapped around them) to prevent further heat loss. Also, remember that children lose heat faster than adults, and thin people lose heat faster than fat people do.

Wearing a life jacket is also a good preventive measure against the gasping reflex. If you fall into cold water, you will automatically gasp for air. If you are facedown in the water you might inhale it, which makes your situation worse.

If you get cold, the first thing that happens is that you start to shiver. As you get colder the shivering increases, and your skin starts to turn red. Later it may turn blue. At this point your core body temperature may have dropped only one degree, but your speech may have become slurred, and your legs and arms may have lost dexterity. You might also feel some pain from the cold.

As your body gets colder, your shivering may slow down or stop. Your body no longer has the energy to try to warm you up. You might appear drunk or confused, and you will be awkward. If you don't get warmed up soon, your muscles will tighten and you may lose consciousness. At this point your pulse will be slow and irregular, your skin may be cold, and your body may be rigid. If you lose consciousness now, you will probably die.

Fortunately, as long as the symptoms are identified in time, hypothermia can be averted. If you find yourself shivering, get out of the cold and into the warm. Drink warm fluids such as hot milk, coffee, or tea (no alcohol). You might want to snuggle into a sleeping bag with a hot-water bottle or some other heat source, or you might want to perform light exercise to warm your body.

If the symptoms are more severe, cut out the exercise, but get warmed up as quickly as possible. You might do this by getting into a sleeping bag between two people and using direct body-to-body contact.

In severe cases, get medical help immediately. In the meantime, avoid jarring the victim. Do not give food or drink, and apply gentle external heat to warm the person. If you are on a boat, get the person into a warm sleeping bag and keep a careful watch on his or her condition. Get professional help immediately; the victim needs to get to a hospital. If the victim has stopped breathing, you may have to apply CPR. In an extreme case, don't assume that the victim is dead. There have been hypothermia victims who regained consciousness in the morgue!

Survival or immersion suits are intended to protect the wearer against hypothermia. In my opinion, few sailors or boaters are likely to need one unless they are working on the ocean commercially and have to be out in all kinds of weather. Survival suits are bulky, and finding a place to stow one onboard an average yacht may be difficult. These suits are best used on larger vessels that may take longer to sink, giving the crew time to get into their emergency gear.

CALLING FOR HELP

If you have a problem onboard your boat that requires outside help, the easiest method is to call the Coast Guard on VHF channel 16 (156.8 MHz). This channel is monitored by both the U.S. and

U.K. Coast Guards. It should be used only to establish contact; then you must switch to another channel. Typically, the Coast Guard will tell you to switch to channel 69, 71, or 78, which are ship-to-shore channels. If you are talking with a Coast Guard ship, you would switch to channels 9, 69, 70, or 72, which are ship-to-ship channels. In the United Kingdom, ship-to-ship channels are 6 and 8, and port operations channels are 12 and 14.

Suppose you are onboard the *Mary One* and initiating a call to another boat called the *Sea Swift*. The procedure is relatively simple. Switch to channel 16 and pick up the mike. Wait for a break in the conversation and then say clearly: "Hello, *Sea Swift*. This is *Mary One*. This is *Mary One*. Over." Repeat your boat's name up to three times.

Sea Swift replies, "Hello, *Mary One*. This is *Sea Swift*. Over."

Your reply should be, "Hello, *Sea Swift*. Go to channel 72 (usually spoken as "channel seven-two"). Over." Then both operators switch to channel 72 to talk. Remember when using the VHF that other people can hear everything you say, and they may be waiting to use the radio.

If you are in an emergency situation you should preface your message with, "Mayday. Mayday. Mayday." Give your boat's position and the nature of the emergency. The Coast Guard will respond and clear the channel of other transmissions. Then they will ask for details of the emergency, an accurate position report, the type of boat, how many people are onboard, and other details.

Remember, Mayday is the most urgent signal you can send. When you broadcast a Mayday signal, you are asking a lot of people to help you, and a large organization swings into action. A bogus message can result in fines or even imprisonment.

A less urgent signal is a Pan signal. You might send this if your boat is dismasted, but not in danger of sinking. In this case transmit the words, "Pan-Pan, Pan-Pan. This is *Mary One*. We have been dismasted." Give your position and tell the Coast Guard if you need assistance. If you only need a tow, they might dispatch a service (such as Sea Tow on the East Coast or Vessel Assist on the West Coast) to pull you home.

There are many courses on safety at sea, and if you intend to learn more about the sport of sailing, you should consider attending one or two. These courses often show how to inflate a life raft, how to stave off hypothermia, how to protect your boat, and how to enjoy the independence of being alone on the ocean.

CHAPTER 10

WEATHER AND YOUR BOAT

As a sailor you must know where the wind is likely to come from and at what strength. You can get this information from weather charts published in newspapers, on Internet sites, or from weather channels on your radio or television. This information will help you decide when and where you will sail. For example, if bad weather is forecast for Sunday afternoon and you really want to go sailing for the weekend, you might make alternate plans to come home Saturday night, or leave early so you won't have to sail in bad conditions. With some care, you can gain a lot of sailing experience without having to weather a storm before you are ready. In fact, I recently talked to one sailor who had sailed nearly forty-five thousand miles between New England and the Caribbean and had seen winds of more than forty-five knots only once. He had obviously picked his weather very carefully.

When you are out sailing, you should tune into weather radio at least once or twice a day to make sure that no bad weather is creeping up on you. You should also keep an eye on the cloud movements and formations. They will tell you a lot about local conditions, often before the weatherman does. If you know that cirrus clouds are indicative of rain within twenty-four to forty-eight hours, you can plan accordingly. If the cirrus clouds have curly tails, often known as mares' tails, warm weather is approaching, and it will rain. If the cirrus is followed by cirrostratus and then altostratus, it indicates the passing of a front and usually a good blow that is typically of short duration. The type and height of the cirrus will give you an idea of what is to come. The passing of a front always comes with a change in the wind direction.

As a sailor you should learn these characteristics of clouds so you will be able to forecast the weather. Here I can only touch on the basics, but I encourage you to find a good book or two and learn more. One I recommend is *Weather for the Mariner* by Rear Admiral Kotsch, U.S. Navy (Ret.), published by the Naval Institute Press. Well-known British weather forecaster Alan Watts has also published a number of books on sailing weather that are worth reading.

CLOUD TYPES

Clouds can be divided into three layers. The very high clouds that are part of the jet stream usually indicate what weather is to come within twenty-four to forty-eight hours. These clouds are generally at eighteen thousand to twenty-five thousand feet. This is where you find cirrus, cirrostratus, and cirrocumulus clouds. Below the high clouds you find the midlevel clouds, seven to eighteen thousand feet. Within this band can be found altostratus and altocumulus. Altostratus clouds appear when a warm front is sliding over a cold front. Usually they bring rain, wind, and poor visibility. The lowest band of clouds range from ground level to seven thousand feet and are usually accompanied by rain. These clouds are stratus, stratocumulus, nimbostratus, cumulus, and cumulonimbus clouds.

High Clouds

Cirrus clouds are thin, wispy clouds, like long streaks painted across the sky with a semidry paintbrush. If the cirrus is very high and moving fast, it usually indicates the onset of a major low (depression). (See Figure 10.1.) If it's scattered, it shows that bad weather is some distance off. If it has curls in the ends, there is a

FIGURE 10.1   Cirrus clouds over Long Island Sound.

warm front coming. If the cirrus lowers and thickens into altostratus, it usually indicates that a warm front is on the way. If it continues to thicken and becomes nimbostratus, expect to see rain and wind—usually a lot of both. (See Figure 10.2.)

Cirrostratus clouds show that warm weather is coming. (See Figure 10.3.) If they are not increasing and are breaking up, you are probably seeing the north or northwestern edge of a low-pressure system. This usually means that the wind will back from southeast to easterly to northeast, depending on how far to the south the low is situated.

Cirrocumulus clouds are white, rippled-looking clouds, which give you the effect of looking at the sun through a gray haze. They usually appear near the end of a storm and indicate good weather to come.

FIGURE 10.2 Rain-bearing stratus clouds are indicative of warm, showery weather with low visibility.

Midlevel Clouds

Altocumulus, when they form high, puffy turrets, are the clouds that accompany thunderstorms. When they lie in bands, it usually means that a warm front with rain is approaching. Altostratus are grayish layers of clouds that often develop when warm air flows over colder air. They frequently signal the approach of rain and foggy weather.

FIGURE 10.3   Cirrostratus clouds indicate that bad weather has passed and the cloud cover is breaking up.

Lower-Level Clouds

Nimbostratus are true rain clouds and may be accompanied by smaller dark gray scudding clouds (pannus) under the layer of gray. Rain is almost continuous in this wet, stormy pattern. Low gray clouds with uniform bases are stratus; they often indicate a lightening breeze. Stratocumulus clouds are usually some of the last clouds you see from storms as they pass. Gradually these clouds fall apart or disappear, leaving good weather behind them. You might also see some heat-generated cumulus clouds where the ocean or land is warmer than nearby areas. Figure 10.4 shows heat-generated cumulus as seen when approaching the Gulf Stream. These are very low clouds that may thicken and become huge thunderheads. When you are out in a sailboat, towering thunderheads with dark, flat bottoms are a signal to head back to harbor.

READING A WEATHER MAP

The weather maps on television or in the newspapers usually show low- and high-pressure systems, fronts, and rain areas. By understanding how wind moves around a front, you can estimate where the wind is likely to be coming from on any given day.

Weather maps show where air masses are located, and it's at the edges of the air masses that most of our weather takes place. When warm air collides with cold air, the collision is marked with a front. If cold air is forcing the warm air out, it's a cold front. If warm air is approaching, it's a warm front (see Figure 10.5).

FIGURE 10.4   Heat-generated cumulus clouds over the Gulf Stream. If these clouds climb high and darken, look out for thunderstorms and sharply veering strong winds.

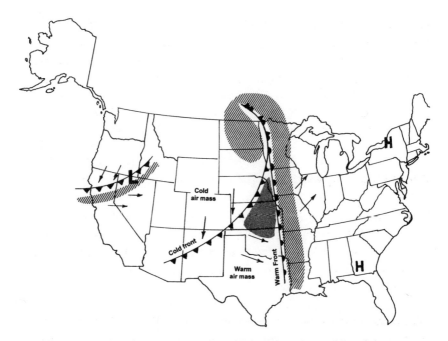

FIGURE 10.5   A warm front stretches down the middle of the country with rain out in front of it. It's followed by a cold front. Where the cold and warm fronts meet, the system becomes an occluded front. Between the warm and cold fronts is an area of fog and drizzle. Notice how the wind direction changes as the front passes through.

If a cold front is colliding with another cold front, you may find that any warm air is forced aloft. In this case, the front is called an occluded front. Usually, but not always, a warm front rides up over a cold front (warm air rises). In almost all cases, unless both air masses are nearly the same temperature, the passing of a frontal system is accompanied by rain, a wind shift, and a change in visibility.

Unless it's weak, a warm front passing through will almost always bring rain, followed by heavier rain, which gives way to drizzle or fog. The rain slows or stops as the front passes, but it may continue as drizzle or fog for a day or two longer. The passing of a warm front is usually accompanied by a large wind shift, typically from south or southwest to north or northwest. The wind usually stays fairly steady after the front has passed, but it may decrease.

As a cold front approaches, you may see some rain or hazy fog in front of it. The wind increases, and may become squally with sudden gusts and ten- to fifteen-degree shifts. Typically, the rain starts just as the front passes. Then it may become heavy, sometimes torrential. When the front has passed, the rain will die out to a few showers or nothing at all. The wind will shift, usually from south or southwest to north or northwest, often becoming fairly gusty; visibility usually becomes extremely clear. When the cold front is strong and there is a large temperature difference between the air masses, you are especially apt to see severe thunderstorms and strong, gusty winds.

For example, after the passing of a strong cold front in Long Island Sound, the wind is from the Connecticut shore and very gusty, with directional shifts of up to twenty degrees. This strong breeze is fun to sail in, but the continual wind shifts and changes in wind speed can tax racing sailors trying to get the very best out of their boats.

LOCAL CONDITIONS

Most sailors sail within forty miles of the coastline—an area affected by local breezes. In spring, when the weather forecasters tell you that coastal areas are likely to be cooler than inland areas, they are right. The ocean temperatures are still in the thirties and forties, while inland temperatures may be in the seventies and eighties. Because the air over the land is warm, it tends to rise. This creates a thermal that draws air in off the ocean toward the warm land. (See Figure 10.6.) The cold ocean air can be drawn in from more than seventy miles at sea, and its speed depends on the air-water temperature differential. In other words, the cooler the water and the warmer the land, the stronger the breeze. In many cases, the late-afternoon sea breeze may be twenty-five knots or more.

You can expect a sea breeze if the water temperature is relatively low, there are few or no clouds, and there is no overlying system pushing wind in the opposite direction of the sea breeze. Sometimes you may find that an overlying system is opposite the sea breeze. For example, we once set sail headed south under spinnaker with the overlying wind out of the north. As we got farther south, we could see a sea breeze on the water well to the south of

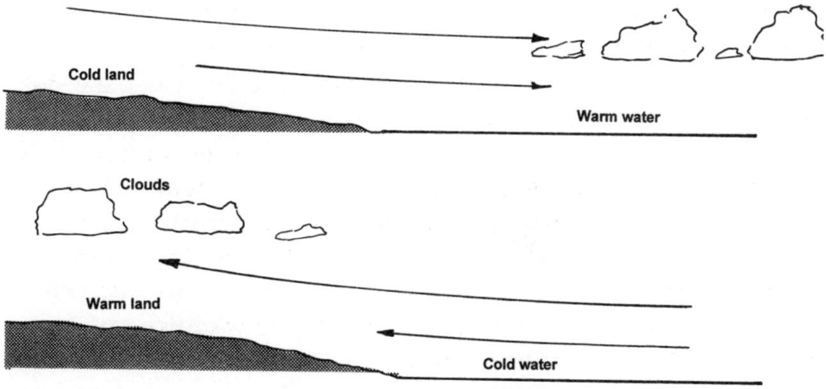

FIGURE 10.6 During warm, sunny days the land heats up rapidly, and air is drawn from the cooler ocean toward the land. Usually, clouds are generated over the land, and a thermal wind results. This happens most often in the spring and early-summer months. At night the land cools down but the water is still fairly warm, so a breeze develops with wind blowing off the land. Land breezes develop most often in late summer and early fall.

us. Boats ahead were losing their spinnakers and setting headsails. It was almost time for us to turn back, so we waited; as the sea breeze came in, we turned the boat 180 degrees without dropping the colorful spinnaker and went home under its power. It isn't often that you can do this. Usually there is an area of flat calm between the coming sea breeze and the overlying wind pattern.

On another occasion in the Solent in England, I saw two racing fleets sailing toward each other, one going east and the other west. Both fleets had spinnakers up, and as they neared each other, the leaders lost all wind. Their sails collapsed. Gradually the leaders made it across the area of calm, and both fleets continued under headsails. In this case, the thermal had developed in the middle of the Solent, and the fleets were able to sail until they ran out of wind.

Sea breezes and frontal systems change the wind direction and herald the onset of rain. They are everyday weather patterns that sailors learn to recognize. But what happens when a major low-pressure system develops? A major low indicates a storm, and although it should be respected, a storm is not necessarily to be feared as long as you know what to do. It's the more devastating storms, such as hurricanes, that sailors fear most.

STORM!

Storm-warning flags have just gone up. A red flag with square black centers means that the average wind speed exceeds thirty-five knots. (Two red flags with black centers indicate a hurricane, whose winds exceed sixty-five knots, or about seventy-four miles per hour.) Your boat is in the water ready for a family picnic to your favorite cove. What should you do? This is the dilemma that faces many sailors, but as long as you are prepared you should be able to handle a storm competently. Your first concern should be for your family's safety. Obviously, you should not start a sailing trip when storm warnings are up. If a hurricane is forecast, find a strongly built structure for your family and take shelter.

Your second concern should be for your boat. What are your options? In a storm you should make sure your boat is tied up and secure. If necessary, add double dock lines and a few more fenders. But an approaching hurricane is another matter. Here you need to take more precautions. Option one is to haul your boat out of the water and truck it to a secure storage area. Option two is to leave your boat in its slip, very heavily secured. Option three is to find a hurricane hole (a sheltered harbor in which you can moor your boat, safely away from the storm's fury) and tie the boat up in it. The speed of the approaching hurricane may determine which option you choose.

Hauling Your Boat

If you own a small boat (less than twenty feet), you should consider hauling it out of the water when a severe storm is forecast. You should certainly haul larger boats. Typically, boats of up to forty feet should be hauled if the wind is likely to be hurricane strength.

As soon as a tropical depression is forecast for a particular area, boatyards start hauling smaller boats. If you want your boat to be among those hauled early, make sure your yard has a standing order for these situations. If your boat is small, have your trailer handy and give the yard a telephone number where you can be reached day or night. When the forecast is upgraded from a tropical depression to a tropical storm, be ready to haul your boat and store it in a secure place. If your boat is less than twenty feet or about the size of the average car, it might fit in a concrete storage building. You can back your boat and trailer into a shed or parking garage, lock the door, and know that your boat is safe. Being first to arrive ensures that you get the pick of the spots. Choose one that is not likely to be flooded during a storm surge or heavy rain.

If your boat is large, you might park it in the lee of a strongly constructed building. But make sure that the boat is tied down securely, both to its trailer and to strong points in the ground. Tie-downs attached to concrete blocks are not strong enough. Boats tied down this way can be blown over in heavy winds. Remember, too, that as a hurricane passes, the wind direction will change, sometimes as much as 180 degrees. So your boat needs to be protected on as many sides as possible. Also remember that parking your boat between two tall buildings can cause other problems. If the wind blows directly between the buildings, it increases in speed up to two or three times, which dramatically increases the pressure on your boat.

When preparing for a storm, every item that causes extra windage should be removed from your boat. Bimini tops, dodgers, roller-furling headsails, awnings, lee cloths, and even dinghies lashed on deck should be removed and stored. Note that the wind speed given for a storm or hurricane is the *average* wind speed. Gusts can be up to thirty miles per hour higher.

WIND PRESSURE Wind pressure increases by the square of the wind's speed. In other words, if a twenty-knot wind exerts four hundred pounds of pressure on your boat, a forty-knot wind will exert sixteen hundred pounds of pressure, and an eighty-knot wind will exert sixty-four hundred pounds of pressure.

Securing Your Boat in Its Slip

This is only an option if the storm is not going to be severe and your slip is reasonably sheltered. If you have a slip in an exposed marina, however, haul your boat or move it to a hurricane hole.

As a first step in securing a boat in a slip, remove every item of extra windage, including roller-furling sails. Next, double your mooring lines and move your boat closer to the middle of the slip. Figure 10.7 shows how it should be moored. Positioning it in the middle with a bit of slack in the ropes gives your boat enough space to rock and roll without riding up over the edge of the dock. Check that your mast (in the case of a sailboat) is not aligned with the mast of a sailboat in an adjacent slip. If both masts lean toward each other, they should not be able to touch. Put fenders out on both sides of your boat to cushion other crafts and keep your boat off the dock.

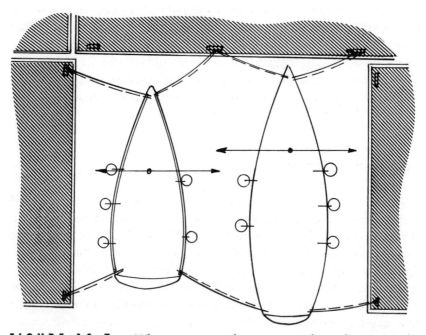

FIGURE 10.7 When stormy weather is expected, two boats in a slip can damage the dock or each other if they are not moored properly. The boats are held away from the slip by breast lines at the stern from boat to boat, and at the bow to the dock. Both boats have fenders out on both sides. The masts are free to move without touching each other.

Then take your dinghy, portable electronics, sails, and loose gear home and stow it all in a basement or garage where it won't get flooded. Also remember that a hurricane surge can run up to eight feet above normal wave heights. Would your marina slips lift off the tops of the pilings if this happened? Try to anticipate these problems and prepare early.

If your boat is on a mooring and you cannot move it, make sure you have doubled up your mooring line. You should also take an additional line from the bow to the mooring chain under the mooring buoy. When a mooring breaks, quite often it's the swivel at the buoy that goes. An extra line fed directly through the chain can give an additional safety factor. Once again, make sure your roller-furling headsails have been removed, along with any other items that may add windage.

Also make sure that the mooring anchors can take the weight of your boat. If the storm surge is eight or ten feet, your boat may be large enough to lift the mooring anchors right off the seabed. If you have any doubts, move to a safer mooring before the storm hits. Put fenders horizontally down the side of your boat in case another boat breaks loose. The fenders may not prevent damage completely, but they will help minimize it. You can also add extra chafe protection to your mooring lines to ensure that they don't break. Then go ashore and watch the storm from your window, not from the deck of your boat.

Finding a Hurricane Hole

If you wait until the storm is nearby before you find a sheltered spot to moor your boat, you may be too late! The time to find a secure hurricane hole is when you are out on your boat during the early summer. At this time you can check out the best locations and figure out where and how you will tie your boat off. When you are looking for a hurricane hole, always ask other sailors or boaters for advice. Then go to the area yourself and inspect it. Make sure your boat can be secured properly if the wind comes from any direction. Check where you may have to lay out an anchor, and where your boat's lines might be taken ashore. Try to imagine the hole with other boats in it and figure out where you would put your own sailboat.

When you head to a hurricane hole before a storm, try to get there as early as possible. If there is more than one boat in it, figure out how the other boats will swing and where you should be located. If the area is really crowded and boats are rafted together (tied to each other), check that masts are free to swing, that all windage is removed, and that the raft has enough ground tackle down. Each boat should have its own anchor, and possibly a second. Yes, the anchors' lines will be a mess to sort out afterward, but at least you'll still have a boat.

At Sea During a Severe Storm or Hurricane

If you cannot get to a hurricane hole or harbor before a major storm is upon you, head for sea and obey the first rule of ocean sailing: Stay away from the "hard stuff" around the edges. The rocks and beaches are only there to keep the ocean in. In really severe weather you are better off a long way out to sea—the farther, the better. Typically, a boat under sail or power will drift up to a hundred miles in a severe storm. On the East Coast, if you can get out beyond the Gulf Stream, your chances of surviving the storm are even better. A storm-force wind against the Gulf Stream will kick up a tremendous short chop and should be avoided at all costs. Depending on your boat, you may decide to run off, to lie hove-to, or to lie to a sea anchor to ride out a severe storm at sea. You need to gain knowledge and experience in handling your boat to decide which of these options is best suited for you and your craft.

Running Off During a Storm or Hurricane   Running off appears to be the most-favored tactic for sailboats with experienced crew onboard. You keep the wind on the quarter and head across the storm. Speed is the factor that you have to be aware of when you are running off. If you go too fast, you may end up broaching the boat and doing serious damage. Before you run off, you need to ascertain where the storm is coming from and where it's going. In one instance, a sailboat ran off directly before a storm and was in bad weather for nearly thirty hours before finally breaking free.

According to the meteorologist who plotted the storm's course, if that boat had headed westward it would have broken out of the storm in four hours.

If the storm is moving due north, the most dangerous quadrant will be the northeastern. This is because the wind speed of the storm and its speed of motion are added together there. You should be aiming to get to the southwesterly quadrant, where the winds will be lower and the sea will probably be smoother.

By keeping the hurricane's winds on your port quarter, you will gradually head toward the easier side of the storm. Typically, wave speeds during a storm are quite high; some authorities suggest twenty to twenty-six miles per hour. If your boat is traveling at similar speeds, you will spend a long time on the crest of a wave and a long time riding the front slope. Just like skiing, as you slide downhill, your boat's speed will increase. Which is okay until you get to the bottom of the wave. Then the boat's bow digs in, and the stern keeps on going. The result? A broach! Often the boat is rolled to its beam ends; sometimes it's rolled over. To help prevent this, your only option is to slow down.

If the boat is going fast without sails, or if the engines are just ticking over, you may want to set a drogue over the stern to slow the boat. How much should you slow it? That depends on your boat and the amount of windage. Ideally, you want to slow your boat's speed to about half to two-thirds of the wave speed. To do this, trail a drogue on a line two hundred to three hundred feet astern of the boat. Skip Raymond of Hathaway, Rieser and Raymond (the manufacturer of the Gale Rider drogue) suggests that by using a bridle, helming chores can be reduced or eliminated; the boat will continue on its own.

But some authorities, such as K. Adlard Coles in his book *Heavy Weather Sailing* and Bernard Moitessier in his book *The Long Way*, suggest that slowing a boat down in a storm is not necessary. In fact, they suggest that faster is better, provided the boat has enough buoyancy to lift the bow after surging down a wave. The only way to know what applies to your boat is to try it and be prepared to change your mind. You should also try a drogue before getting into heavy weather to make sure that you know how to handle it when a storm comes calling.

Heaving-To Heaving-to is another option when weathering a severe storm at sea. It's a way to stop the boat and give the crew time to rest. Heaving-to is done by backing the jib. The mainsail is set as normal; the helm may need to be put down and tied off. The jib is taken to windward and sheeted in. The theory is that the mainsail is driving the boat, while the headsail is stopping it. If the two sails counteract each other properly, the boat will stay hove-to. Heaving-to is best done with a boat that has a reasonably long keel. Short-keeled boats will heave-to if their sails are in balance, but they tend to get a little squirrelly in large waves. When setting up to heave-to, try to keep both sails close together near the center of the boat, rather than spread apart, where a wave may unbalance the boat and cause it to broach or be thrown onto its beam ends. In my opinion, heaving-to is a good strategy in winds up to about force six, but beyond that the boat becomes vulnerable to being knocked beam-on by the wind and sea. Being beam-on to a strong gale is not a good situation to be in, because you can be rolled over by a breaking sea.

Setting a Sea Anchor Setting a sea anchor is a second way to give the crew some rest during a storm or hurricane. A sea anchor is always set off the bow of the boat with two hundred to three hundred yards of line. This length is needed to give some shock absorbency to the line, and to allow the sea anchor to sink deep enough in the seas. Too short a line could pull the sea anchor above the sea surface and collapse it. Sea anchors seem to be very effective for multihulls, and reasonably effective for monohulls and powerboats. But when you set a sea anchor or heave-to in a storm, the boat is moving backward at about one to two knots, and damage can be done to the rudder.

The idea behind a sea anchor is that it puts the bow of your boat into the wind and keeps the boat bow-on to the wind and sea. If your boat gets beam-on, there's a good possibility that it will capsize. Powerboats lying to a sea anchor need to make sure that any large forward-facing windows are protected. Imagine what it would be like inside the boat if one of these windows were to break in severe weather.

Chafe   No matter where you put your boat in a storm, one thing that is going to give you major problems is chafe. Mooring lines need to be protected against chafe, as do drogue lines, sea-anchor rodes (lines), and any other lines used to hold the boat in a fixed position. To reduce chafe, your lines should be passed through a flexible plastic or canvas pipe. Hold the chafe pipe securely in place by tying a length of thin line through it, then splicing the line into your anchor rope. If you don't have a length of plastic pipe, use rags or seizing (small-diameter rope wrapped around the line to stop it from chafing) to protect your lines, and shorten the line after it has chafed in one spot for a few hours.

Protecting your boat against bad weather begins long before a storm is in sight. It starts when you scope out the best place to shelter your boat during a storm, or when you purchase extra dock lines and talk to your neighbor about arranging your dock so that both boats survive. It also begins as you try out a drogue or sea anchor when the wind is blowing at fifteen knots, or your engines are ticking over. If you habitually spend time offshore, be it on a sailboat or on a powerboat, you should familiarize yourself with sea anchors and drogues and how they can be best fitted on your boat. In doing so, you will learn more about your boat and your nautical skills.

Your boat should survive the hurricane season with these few simple precautions. Enjoy your sailing, but remember that there will always be another hurricane. Your preparations should start early.

CHAPTER 11

BUYING YOUR FIRST BOAT

What do you want in your first boat? A dinghy for frostbite racing? A small cruising boat? A large cruising boat? No matter what you're seeking, look carefully at the market to get the best boat for your money. But how do you know what is the best boat for you? This is a difficult question if you don't know a lot about boats. You need to develop a strategy for assessing boats before you buy one.

ASSESSING YOUR NEEDS

This strategy should take into account where you intend to sail, what you want to do with your boat, and what sailing experience you have. You might decide that you enjoy singlehanding, or that you want to sail around the world. You might be determined to become a racing sailor, or to cruise offshore. These goals are achievable, but your first boat should be aimed at helping you gain experience in relatively benign coastal waters. When you have a year or two of experience, you can go world traveling. It's relatively easy to sell a boat, so you don't need to buy your globe-girdling sloop yet. Buy one that is suitable for your current sailing style, and when your knowledge and experience increase, sell it and buy a more advanced vessel.

Where Do You Sail?

Your first step in assessing your boat-buying needs is to decide where you want to sail. If you want to cruise Puget Sound, it would be difficult to cover a lot of ground in one weekend unless you have a high-speed powerboat. On a low-speed sailboat, you would have to make the trip in easy stages. Remember that a displacement sailboat can only travel so far in one hour. In general, Froude's law applies. If your boat has a twenty-five-foot waterline, its absolute maximum speed is $1.5 \sqrt{LWL}$, which is 7.5 knots ($1.5 \sqrt{25} = 7.5$). Usually your speed would be about five or six knots, because going flat-out strains the boat and gear. So if you only want to sail for three to four hours each day, your range is fifteen to twenty nautical miles. In contrast, a planing powerboat might have a top speed of forty miles per hour, and a cruising speed of thirty-two miles per hour. Its cruising range would be close to a hundred miles for a three-hour trip. In such ways, where you plan to sail helps determine the type and size of boat you want.

What Is Your Sailing Style?

Deciding where you cruise also helps establish your sailing style. For example, if you cruise the bayou country, you might simply sail from one port to another, have a meal ashore, and the following morning cruise back to your home port. This tells you that you may not want to cook much onboard; a microwave will do instead of a complete galley. Similarly, you should decide whether you plan to shower onboard, or if you can just as well shower in a marina where you regularly sail.

WHAT ARE THE MAXIMUM SPEED AND RANGE OF MY BOAT?

Froude said that a displacement-hull boat can travel at a theoretical maximum speed of $1.34\sqrt{LWL}$. In actual fact, sailboats have overhangs that help increase the maximum speed, so $1.5\sqrt{LWL}$ is probably a more accurate number. So if a boat has a waterline of twenty-five feet, its theoretical maximum speed will be about 7.5 knots. This means that if you want to go twenty miles at maximum speed, it will take you about 2.67 hours ($20 \div 7.5$). But most boats don't travel at maximum speed; it puts too much strain on the engine and gear. Instead, they operate at a cruising speed, which might be around six knots. In this case, your trip will take 3.33 hours. Figure 11.1 shows how to apply Froude's law.

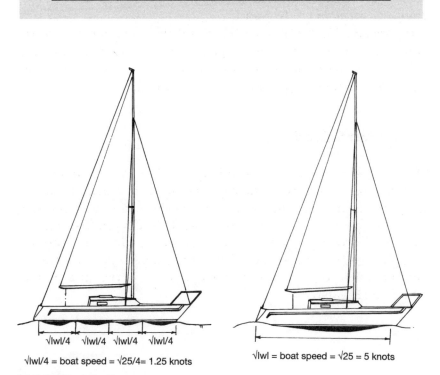

$\sqrt{lwl}/4$ $\sqrt{lwl}/4$ $\sqrt{lwl}/4$ $\sqrt{lwl}/4$

$\sqrt{lwl}/4$ = boat speed = $\sqrt{25}/4$ = 1.25 knots

$\sqrt{lwl}$ = boat speed = $\sqrt{25}$ = 5 knots

FIGURE 11.1

Another decision is how often you plan to anchor. If you moor in a marina you can walk ashore, but if you anchor off you will need to carry a dinghy (unless you can schedule a launch service). How many people you plan to have onboard is equally important, because this number determines how many bunks you will need. And how often will you be sailing shorthanded? Frequent shorthanded sailing can affect the gear you need to buy. Do you intend to do your own maintenance or have the yard do it for you? If you are a do-it-yourselfer, you probably want a low-maintenance boat that won't detract too much from your sailing time. All these decisions affect the type of boat that is best for you. The Sailing Trial (page 168) lists more decisions you should make before buying a boat.

WHERE TO LOOK FOR BOATS

Having assessed your needs, it's time to make a foray into the world of yacht brokers, boat dealers, and boatbuilders. Depending on whether you intend buying a small or large boat, new or used, your experience will be different. If you intend to purchase a small boat—say, less than twenty feet—you are probably better off looking in magazines and checking out boats you find listed there. Most yacht brokers do not handle small boats, since the investment of their time and effort is simply not remunerative enough. Neither are small boats listed on the brokers' equivalent of the multiple listing service. Only for midsized or larger boats (around twenty-eight feet and up) might you go through a broker.

The new-versus-used decision also affects where you will look for a boat. For a new boat you should get brochures, usually from a dealer specializing in the type of boat you want. You can also look through magazines and go to boat shows. Any of these approaches will tell you what is available in your size and price range. For a used boat you can go to a yacht broker and follow his or her advice. In general, you get more when you buy a used boat, provided it's in good condition. Also, you may find several used boats of the same model, in which case you can check them all out and bid on the best one.

If you decide to buy a new boat, a survey is not quite as important as it is for a used one. As marine surveyor Bob Wallstrom of

Blue Hill, Maine, points out, if you are buying one of the first few boats off a production line it pays to get it surveyed, but if the production line has been in existence for a long time, you may not need a survey. When buying a very small boat, you can make your own survey or ask a knowledgeable friend to help you.

Buying a Used Boat Through a Yacht Broker

There are hundreds of boats listed in the brokerage pages of most sailing magazines. When you spot one that interests you, call the broker who is handling it. You do not need to call several yacht brokers; these professionals are all connected by a service similar to the multiple-listing service used by Realtors. Find a broker whom you like and trust. When I needed information on several boats, I called Scott Heckard at Annapolis Sailyard in Maryland. He sent me a magnificent package of information, and then called to make sure I had everything I needed. This type of response is rare, so I recommend him to anyone for help when buying a boat.

Going to the right broker is important, because a broker can also help you *sell* your first boat when you decide to trade up. Brokers like repeat clients. A broker with whom you have worked for a few years will keep you informed about good buys that have just appeared on the market, and will be able to make an intelligent assessment of your boat when the time comes to sell it. You might think that the boat you are buying will last you forever, but someday you may want to sell it and get a larger or later model.

Initially, you will need to tell a broker about size and price range, what you want to do with the boat, and where you want to sail it. Note also that most boat brokers don't deal with boats of less than about twenty-four feet. (Typically, an eighteen- to twenty-four-footer is a first boat for many sailors.) He or she will probably ask if you are willing to travel to inspect a boat, whether you can negotiate up or down, and other pertinent details. The broker might ask where you intend to keep the boat and whether you have a slip or mooring. Don't be offended by the number and variety of questions a broker asks. As yacht broker Jeff Rice of J.C. Rice International, in Saunderstown, Rhode Island, says, brokers are only trying to get a feel for your tastes and styles so that they can match you up with the ideal boat. The more they know about what you want, the more accurately they can work for you.

How do you know that the price you are being asked to pay for a boat is a fair one? You don't, unless you compare a lot of prices and equipment lists for the same type of boat. If you buy a used boat, you should always get it surveyed unless it's a small dinghy or less than twenty feet. There are no other exceptions to this rule. To see if you really want to invest in a survey, check out the points listed in the mini survey shown in The Sailing Trial on page 168. If a boat passes these tests and you decide that you still want to buy it, then invest in a survey.

If you have to put your money up before a surveyor has inspected the boat, buy it subject to survey. If you are buying a boat with a large inboard engine or a generator, you may need to get an engine mechanic to make sure the machinery is in good order. This should be done in addition to the survey. Most surveyors are not engine mechanics and will not survey engines. I recommend surveyors that belong to the National Association of Marine Surveyors (NAMS). To be certified by NAMS, surveyors go through an eight-hour exam and then have to perform a test survey, which is reviewed by a panel of NAMS surveyors to make sure it's up to standard.

Usually, when you find a boat that you like and want to make an offer, you go through the broker. On making the offer, the broker usually requires 10 percent of the boat price to ensure that you intend to go through with the purchase. This 10 percent is put in an escrow account until the deal is made or collapses. Only after the boat is surveyed should you put up more money. Brokers will also handle all the paperwork required when you buy a boat, but most do not handle documentation, taxes, or registration. That is left up to the new owner.

Another feature you should consider when buying a boat is its resale value. Let's assume that you want to sell it again in three years. Take a look at the value of boats from the same manufacturer that are three years older than the one you are purchasing. Figure out how much the price has risen or fallen, and add or subtract this from the cost of your boat. While there is no guarantee that your boat will gain or lose the same amount, this calculation will at least give you some indication.

Buying a New Boat

When you set out to buy a new boat, you do not usually go to a yacht broker. Like buying your own car, you go out and kick tires (or should I say keels?). The first step is the same as before, however, in that you should decide on a budget and determine where you are going to sail. Then go to boat shows, visit local dealers, and check out advertisements in sailing magazines. Your primary purpose at this stage is to get brochures and inventory lists so that you can figure out the type of boat you can afford.

COMPARING BOATS

The next step in the process is to compare boats. Never buy the first vessel that strikes your fancy. You need to weigh one option against another, getting a feel for their relative costs and merits. Begin by looking at a few numbers.

Looking at the Numbers

To get a feel for performance, you can use the sail area:displacement ratio and the displacement:length ratio. Assume that in light winds, a boat's wetted surface (wetted surface is directly related to frictional drag) is related to its displacement, and that the sail area is used to push each pound of displacement through the water. You can see that performance in light winds is related to the sail area:displacement ratio. The higher this number, the better the boat will perform in lighter winds.

You know that according to Froude's law, a boat's potential maximum speed is related to its waterline length. But comparing waterline lengths will always show that the longer boat is faster. So use the displacement:length ratio to nondimensionalize the number. This enables you to compare the relative speed potential boats of slightly different lengths.

It's usually impossible to get a number for a boat's stability from builders or designers. So you can use a number obtained from a capsize study done after the Fastnet disaster. This number, known as the capsize factor, should be less than 2 for most boats.

For boats that are going to sail close inshore, the number can be slightly higher than 2, but not much.

I also use two other numbers to get an idea of how much fresh water and fuel are onboard. The fresh water:displacement and the fuel:displacement ratios show what percentage of a boat's displacement is fresh water and what percentage is fuel. In general, I find that cruising boats have a fresh water:displacement ratio of more than 5 percent, with more cruising-oriented boats often near 7 percent, and racing boats at 1 to 2 percent. When it comes to the fuel:displacement ratio, most cruising boats come in at 3 to 5 percent and racing boats at around 1 percent.

The Sailing Trial

Now that you have decided on a short list of new boats, ask for a sailing trial. This should tell you a little bit more about them and help make the final decision. Rather than sit back and enjoy the cruise, there are a number of things you should do on a sailing trial. These range from checking the way sails are handled to examining visibility when you return to the dock. Here's a list of twenty points to check over when you are onboard. You may find more as you go through the boat.

1. When you step aboard the boat, see how fenders and dock lines are tied on. If you like to tie them to a cleat and there is no cleat, this may be a source of irritation while you own this boat.
2. Help set the sails rather than letting the salesperson do it. This way you can make sure the halyards and leads are led properly. See how difficult it is to raise and lower the sails on your own.
3. Make sure that you and your spouse or partner can move around the boat easily, both below and above deck. If you have children, make sure that they have comfortable bunks and a place to stow their toys.
4. Start the engine and check the control locations. See if they suit the way you sail, and be sure that you do not have to reach through the steering wheel to adjust them.

5. When the boat is under sail, go below and check out the handholds to see if they are in the locations where you need them. Check out the galley when the boat is heeled to port and to starboard. You may find that the stove does not swing properly, or that you cannot get into the icebox on one tack.

6. Check the bilges to see if the bilge pump can draw (suck water) when the boat is heeled.

7. Check the head and the galley sinks to see if they backfill when the boat is heeled. Check the cockpit also to see if the drains backfill.

8. When steering, get a feel for the weight of the helm. If you have a lot of helm in eight to ten knots of wind, you may not be able to hold the boat in twenty knots, or you may have to reef early. Try to get a feel for the sensitivity of the helm and whether the boat is quick to respond.

9. If the boat has ground tackle, see that it works properly without binding or hanging up. Untangling a snarl every time you use the anchor won't be much fun.

10. When coming back into the dock, check the visibility from the helm location. If you cannot see the dock very well, you may have difficulty bringing the boat alongside.

11. Check the way the boat is rigged; be sure that you can tune or make minor repairs on the mast if you need to. Complicated masts may be expensive for a yard to set up and tune.

12. All halyards should be rope. There is no need to use wire halyards on boats now that special low-stretch ropes (called Spectra or similar names) have been designed.

13. Make sure you can comfortably get in and out of the forehatch if required—especially if you have to change the sail by lifting it through the forehatch. Also check all the lockers to make sure that you can easily get gear in and out.

14. Check below decks for noise levels when the engine is running. You can buy an inexpensive decibel meter at Radio Shack to check noise levels. The reading should not be higher than seventy-five, or so loud that you cannot carry on a normal conversation. High noise levels can lead to fatigue and eventual loss of hearing.

15. When docking the boat, check which way the stern swings when you put the boat astern. You may find that this direction of swing helps dock the boat—or it may make docking more

difficult. Most sterns swing to port (or left) when you put the boat astern. Also, see how responsive the rudder is when the boat is moving astern. Most have a poor response until the boat is moving fairly fast astern.

16. Check items such as cleats and other deck fittings. Sharp-cornered cleats or toe rails can saw through dock lines in a single season unless special chafe-prevention measures are taken.

17. Check how easy it is to get on and off the boat. If you normally board your boat from a dinghy, borrow one and try to board this boat.

18. If you can find out how much fuel the engine uses over a period of time, you can estimate how much fuel you will require for a weekend or a season. You can also get a feeling for how long a tank of fuel will last and how much range the boat has under power.

19. Check each piece of deck gear to make sure it's located where it's easy to handle, and that items such as rope tails and winch handles are reachable. For example, a winch may be placed on the cabin top next to the companionway and under the dodger, but when the handle is inserted in the winch, it cannot be turned because the dodger is in the way. Check also that lockoffs are properly positioned, in line with the winch and the turning block.

20. Talk to owners of similar boats to find out if a particular problem plagues this make. For example, a friend wanted to buy a particular boat. After inspecting a number of boats, he learned that the rudder bearings jammed and the bearing housing rattled when the rudder was gently shaken. Replacing the bearings was an option, but would cost more than he was willing to spend.

BUYING NEW SAILS

I once had a client come to me and complain that his boat had been able to beat a sister ship last season; this season, however, he found it impossible to catch this other boat. What was wrong with his boat? I went through the usual list of suspects. Was the boat's bottom clean? Yes. Was the mast in the same place as last year? Yes. In fact, the client had tuned it himself to exactly the tape marks from last year. Was the boat the same weight? Yes. Was he sheeting the sails properly? Yes. Now I was stumped. What else could be causing the problem? "Are there any changes between your boat and your sister ship that I don't know about?" I asked him. "Well," I was told, "the sister ship did get a new mainsail last winter."

Lights came on. "How old is your mainsail?" I asked. It turned out that my client had bought it when he purchased the boat, in the fall of 1979. The mainsail was nearly twenty years old!

I asked to look at the mainsail. Sure enough, all the telltale marks of wear and fatigue were there. The corner rings were stretched. At each corner the stitching was also stretched, and wrinkles had begun radiating outward. The leach and foot were loose and flapping. Stitches showed obvious signs of breakage, and in many places had been resewn. Battens fitted in the pockets very loosely where the pockets had stretched. When the mainsail was set, it became very baggy and took a lot of tension before it flattened out. In fact, the halyard had to be hauled so tight it seemed like it was going to break. And this wasn't in heavy winds!

When I was with an America's Cup campaign, we learned that sails start to lose their performance edge after about a hundred hours of sailing. This sail had seen more than two hundred hours of sailing in its first season, and it had been used for twenty more seasons since. My advice was to buy a new mainsail. The owner did so, and now he can keep up with the sister ship once again.

Buying sails is expensive. How do you keep the costs down? One way is to make sure you place a sail order in the fall or winter to take advantage of any special rates the sailmaker offers. In spring sailmakers work flat-out getting sails ready and they charge full price, but in the winter they are often short of work and offer deals to keep clients coming in the door. You may be able to get a sail up to 20 percent cheaper if you are prepared to order in the winter. Often offering cash in advance will also help lower the price.

If you own a cruising boat and have no intention of going racing, you can buy Dacron sails without any of the special high-strength fabrics that push prices up. If you have roller furling, get a headsail with a UV protection trip on the leach. This will help prolong the life of your sail. Treat your sail gently. Don't just cram it down the hatch and walk all over it. Put it away in the sail bag at the end of each trip, and stow it below or in the sail locker. If a storm is forecast, drop the roller-reefed sail and stow it below. Storms seem to like to unfurl roller-furled sails and flog them to death.

Another precaution to prolong the life of your sails is to check throughout the forward part of the boat and the mast, taping over any sharp edges. This will help prevent snagging a sail and tearing it. And don't let sails flog any more than necessary. Flogging reduces the life of your sails.

WHAT TO DO WITH YOUR BOAT WHEN YOU GO HOME

You've had a great day sailing and its time to go home. What should you do with the boat? First, make sure it's washed down with fresh water and tied off securely, either in a marina slip or on a mooring. Second, make sure everything is turned off—the battery, the gas, and the self-powered navigation instruments. Third, make sure it's thiefproof. In other words, when you stand on the dock just before leaving, take a walk around the deck to be sure the hatches are tightly closed, the sails are put away, and the sail bin is locked. If electronics are visible, draw the blinds. This will prevent a potential thief from seeing your equipment; it will also help keep sunlight from warming the interior.

Take all perishable items home with you; they will rapidly rot if left in the boat. When you leave your boat, remember that summer daytime temperatures can reach ninety degrees. Temperatures inside the cabin could reach well over a hundred.

You should also leave the refrigerator or icebox lid ajar so that air can circulate. And it's a good idea to leave locker doors tied open. (Don't just leave them ajar; they will bang back and forth as wakes from other boats make your boat roll.) Ventilation is important in a boat that will be left at the dock all week. If the boat has a WC, flush it with the remainder of the soapy wash-down water, and once per season add a little lanolin to the flushing mixture to lubricate the seals.

Taking Your Boat With You

In general, boats of less than twenty-four feet can be hauled and kept at home to reduce dockage or mooring fees. This will also reduce wear and tear on your boat, and you won't have to paint the bottom quite so often.

If you haul your boat out after sailing it—known as dry-sailing—you will need either a crane or a trailer. Typically, you will either paddle or motor your boat up to the trailer and float it on, or use a crane to lift it out of the water and place it on chocks or on a trailer. Once the boat is out of the water, it should be washed down with soapy water to get rid of the salt. Salt is hydroscopic and will absorb moisture. This keeps your boat damp all week, and before too long it will smell and look like it's in poor shape. If you can, you should also wash off your sails with fresh water so that they will not mildew.

Remember that driving home at sixty to seventy miles an hour subjects your boat to the equivalent of a hurricane. Before leaving the shore, remove items such as the bimini top or dodger that could get damaged by high winds. Make sure that you lower all antennaes and secure loose gear. A loose winch handle can cause a lot of damage if it slides and bounces around inside the boat.

If you have been sailing on fresh water, simply sponge the boat off with soapy water. When you get home, open any lockers and cabinets inside the hull to allow them to air out. Open the icebox and leave the lid askew to allow air to circulate.

Note, too, that when you dry sail-your boat, you should use a bottom paint that can dry out. The surface layer of some bottom paints oxidizes when the boat is lifted out of the water; it's then ineffective when the boat is put back into the water. A good bottom paint for a boat that is dry-sailed is Interlux's Micron CSC Extra. It can be repeatedly dunked and dried and will continue to work well.

CHAPTER 12

SAILING AWAY

s Water Rat said to Mole in Kenneth Grahame's *Wind in the Willows*, "There is nothing—absolutely nothing—half so much worth doing as simply messing about in boats." That comment was written in 1908 and still holds true today.

Having read through this book, you are probably wondering if you should make the next step and call a sailing school. I urge you to do just that. If you got this book for Christmas and it's snowing outside, you can call Offshore Sailing School or J World—to name two of the best-known schools that operate out of Florida and other warm climates—and enjoy a warm-weather vacation while you learn a new skill. This skill will stay with you for the rest of your life. If you got this book at just about any other time of the year, a sailing school near you may be open and looking to help you get afloat.

Once you have learned to sail, you can teach your entire family and enjoy a family-afloat lifestyle. Learning to sail is not a game like golf or football that you leave your family to play. Sailing is a family sport. All of you can board a boat on a Friday evening and head for a new destination. You can enjoy going to places you've never been before by sea. This keeps your children where you can see them—where they can enjoy your company and learn new skills and confidence. The confidence gained handling any type of crisis at sea will stand them in good stead for the remainder of their lives. They can also learn about places and people.

When I am entering a new port, especially one that I have read about in a book, I wonder what it was like for the early seamen to enter a strange land. Transport yourself back to the fifteenth century. Sir Francis Drake has just sailed across the Atlantic for the first time and landed on the isthmus of Panama, where he climbed a tree and saw the Pacific Ocean for the first time. He vowed to sail in that ocean one day. What must it have been like for him to step ashore there, not knowing what to expect? Drake later sailed around Cape Horn and is rumored to have reached the coast of Oregon in 1577–80. He finished the voyage by sailing west across the Pacific, rounding the Cape of Good Hope, then returning to England having circumnavigated the world. Imagine him arriving at each new island; wondering if the people were friendly; making such a voyage in a ship that was only about a hundred tons displacement, cooped up with eighty or more other men for over two years while they headed westward?

You might not get the same thrill and wonderment as Drake, but you can enjoy sailing into a port you have never seen before. Just making the journey is half the fun. The other half is exploring a new port or town.

Also, being on a boat offers more pleasures than just sailing. You can raft up with friends and enjoy the camaraderie. A sailboat also moves at just the right speed to troll for many kinds of fish. I have caught bluefish, striped bass, small sharks, and many other types of fish from the back of a sailboat. If the fish is not to your liking, simply release it and it goes on its way. You can also swim from your boat (make sure you can get back aboard *before* going swimming). Some sailors take along sailboards or boogie boards for use when the boat is at anchor; others take snorkeling gear and enjoy the underwater sights.

There are many things you can do on your boat, from reading to your favorite hobbies. I know of one sailor who uses his boat as his office and home. He has a portable computer, cell phone, and modem and does most of his work directly from his boat. What you do with your boat is limited only by your imagination. Start sailing and expand your horizons and enjoyment.

Good luck, and may the wind always be fair.

GLOSSARY

Abeam: To one side of the boat at ninety degrees to the centerline of the vessel.

Aft: Toward the stern of the boat.

Alee: On the leeward or downwind side of the boat.

Anchor: A method of parking your boat when there are no buoys or docks to tie up to. It entails throwing a heavy metal anchor over the side. The anchor can be one of several types, depending on the type of bottom.

Apparent wind: The wind that you feel when your boat is moving. For example, if the wind were blowing from astern at twenty knots and your boat were sailing at five knots, the apparent wind would be fifteen knots. If you stopped your boat, you would feel a full twenty knots of wind. This wind would then be the true wind. When you are sailing to windward, the apparent wind is calculated from the angle at which you are sailing into the wind, the wind speed, your boat's speed, and its leeway angle.

Apparent wind angle: The angle that the apparent wind makes with the bow of the boat. Typically, on a twelve-meter (39.2-foot) vessel this angle will be about thirty degrees. On a cruising boat it might be about thirty-five to forty degrees.

Babystay: The innermost wire or rod running from the mast to the deck on the front of the mast.

Backstay: A wire or rod used to hold the mast in place. It runs from the stern to the top of the mast and is usually permanently fixed.

Beam: The transverse distance across your boat.

Beam reach: When the apparent wind is blowing from ninety degrees to the centerline of your boat.

Bearing: The angle at which an object bears relative to your boat. For example, you might say that a lighthouse bears 240 degrees.

Belly: The middle of a sail.

Bermuda race: A race of about 620 miles from Newport to Bermuda held every two years in even-numbered years. The Marion-Bermuda race is for cruising sailors and is held in odd-numbered years.

Boatyard: An expensive place you go to get the broken gear on your boat fixed.

Boom: You might think that this is the sound the spar makes when it clunks you on the head during a tack or gibe, but it isn't. It's the horizontal spar at the bottom of the mainsail.

Bowline: A knot used by sailors to tie almost everything to almost everything else. It's easy to tie (after you have learned how to do it) and easy to undo.

Broad reach: When the apparent wind is blowing from abaft the beam but not over the stern. In other words, when the wind is blowing from about 3:30 to 5:30 on the hands of a clock, assuming 12:00 is the bow. Another way to describe a beam reach might be that it occurs when the wind is blowing at 100 to 170 degrees, if the bow of the boat is at 0 degrees.

Buoy: Buoys mark the edges of channels in fairly deep water. As the water gets shallower, a post may be used. Buoys may be of several types. (See text for details.)

Capsize: When the boat tips over to ninety degrees or more.

Catamaran: A twin-hulled sailing vessel originally developed by Polynesians.

Chartering: After you have learned to sail, you can charter a boat anywhere in the world. Bareboat chartering is the most common method. When you charter bareboat, you supply the food, drink, crew, and just about everything else. A crewed charter is more expensive, but you are treated like royalty.

Checkstay: A part of the running backstay used to fine-tune part of the mast below the running backstay attachment point. It is used to stop the mast from bowing forward when the running backstay is tightened.

Cleat: A piece of gear used for stubbing toes. Well, not really. Cleats are used to fasten a rope. They can be jam, cam, or conventional and will hold ropes under most loads.

Clew: The aftmost bottom corner of a sail. It's also the corner at the junction of the foot and the leach.

Closehauled: Sailing to windward as closely as possible. Typically a boat sailing closehauled will sail at an angle of about forty-five degrees to the true wind direction, which translates into thirty to thirty-five degrees of apparent wind angle.

Close reach (or close fetch): When the boat is sailing neither closehauled nor with the wind abeam. The closer to closehauled you are sailing, the more of a close reach you are sailing on.

Clove hitch: A knot used to tie ropes to a round object. It can be unrolled if a lot of tension is put on the line.

COLREGS: Short for *International Rules for the Prevention of Collisions at Sea.*

Current: Any consistent movement of water. A tidal current can be created when the tide comes in or goes out. There are also major currents such as the Gulf Stream created by oceanic rotation.

Depth sounder: A piece of electronic gear that tells you how deep the water is. It usually sounds an alarm just before you hit the rocks.

Dinghy: A small boat that may be sailed, rowed, or driven by a motor.

Downwind: Sailing in the direction of the wind.

Draft: The depth of your boat in the water.

Drag: The resistance of a boat moving through the water is sometimes known as its drag. (See *resistance.*)

EPIRB: Emergency Position Indicating Response Beacon. You start an EPIRB when the boat sinks to tell searchers where you are.

Fastnet: A lighthouse off the southwestern corner of Ireland. Racing sailors set out from Cowes, on the Isle of Wight, to sail around the Fastnet light and back to Plymouth in Devon, England. The distance is about 625 miles.

Fender: The rubber tube that you put between the boat and the dock to prevent the boat from being damaged as it comes alongside. *Warning:* Do not use your limbs as a fender. Your eyes will water strongly afterward.

Fog signals: Sounds made in thick fog. Usually a bell, gong, horn, or whistle is used.

Foot: The bottom of a sail.

Gaff rig: A four-sided sail with a gaff boom at the top of the sail.

Genoa: A large headsail that overlaps the mast.

Gibing: When the boat is turned so that the wind passes across its stern.

GPS (Global Positioning System): A satellite-based navigation system that allows you to go anywhere in the world without learning how to use a sextant or sight reduction tables.

Gulf Stream: A major ocean current flowing from the Gulf of Mexico and around the north Atlantic. It is usually detected by measuring the temperature of the ocean water.

Gunkholing: Exploring shallow waters and interesting coves with your boat. Quite often you'll go aground where nobody can find you and will have to wade ashore through thick mud to get help.

Gust: A puff of wind. Experienced sailors can see a gust of wind moving across the water toward them by observing the water's surface. A gust shows itself when local wavelets create a dark patch of water.

Guy: A rope used to control a spinnaker pole. Sometimes called an after- or foreguy.

Halyard: The rope used to hoist the sail.

Head: The top corner of a sail, or the top edge of a square sail. *Head* can also refer to the toilet compartment aboard a boat.

Header: A wind that blows directly into the bow of the boat. The conventional response to a header is to stand into the wind and then tack in an effort to use the momentum of the shift.

Headstay: The forwardmost wire running from the mast to the deck at the bow. On cruising boats it might have a roller furling gear fitted on it.

Hypothermia: Loss of body temperature that can result in death.

In irons: When the boat is head-to-wind with the sails flapping. Typically, the boat is unable to move and is being blown slowly backward.

Jib: A headsail that does not overlap the mast. When you buy a new boat, you might get a mainsail and a working jib—that is, a general-purpose jib—with the purchase.

Junk rig: A sail plan used by junks in the Far East. It's easy to reef and to stow.

Knockdown: When the boat is tipped over to about ninety degrees and comes back upright.

Laminar flow: Flow next to a hull or sail that is very smooth and has low resistance. In light winds sailors try to move gently on their boats in order to maintain laminar flow as far as possible along the hull. Laminar flow only extends a few millimeters from the hull.

Leach: The trailing edge of any sail.

Leeboard: A board that is fitted to the outside of the hull (usually there's one on each side) to help stop the boat from sliding sideways, or making leeway. A leeboard can usually be raised to reduce wetted surface and help the boat go faster. These are features of older vessels and rarely seen today. (See also *leeway*.)

Leecloth or **leeboard:** To keep you from falling out of a bunk, a leecloth is fastened to the bunk's bottom and tied along the bunk's side. The leecloth can also be made of a sheet of plywood; then it's known as a leeboard.

Leeway: When a boat slides sideways when it's intended to go forward. Most boats make a slight angle of leeway (about five to ten degrees) to enable the keel to generate lift and help the boat sail almost into the wind.

Lift: Lift is generated when a foil or wing is placed at an angle of incidence to the direction that the wind is coming from. For example, an airplane wing generates lift to keep it flying. On a boat, both the sails and the keel (centerboard, leeboard, or daggerboard) generate lift when the boat is sailing to windward.

Luff: The front or leading edge of any sail. When used as a verb, it means that the boat is turned slightly into the wind. If the boat is brought all the way into the wind and stopped, it may be said that "the boat was luffed head-to-wind."

Mainsail: The sail set on the back of the main mast on sloops and ketches. On schooners it is the sail set on the aftermost mast.

Mainsheet: The rope used to control the position of the mainsail.

Marina: An expensive place to park your boat while you earn enough money to support it.

Masthead light: A light at the top of the mast, usually used to light up masthead wind instruments. Some boats have a strobe light a the top of the mast for emergency use.

Midstay: The middle stay in the forward part of the boat running from the mast to the deck.

MSD (Marine Sanitation Device): Coast Guard term for the head.

Multihull: Any boat with more than one hull. Catamarans and tri-marans are multihulls.

Neap tides: These tides occur when the sun and moon are in opposition to each other and have the smallest rise and fall.

Optimist: A small dinghy used to teach children to sail. There are regional, national, and world championships for Optimist sailors.

Outhaul: The rope or wire used to tighten the foot of the mainsail.

PFD (Portable Flotation Device): Coast Guard terminology for a Coast Guard–approved life jacket.

Port: A place where you can leave your boat—but large ships also use ports, and tend to make large waves that rock your boat. *Port* also refers to the left-hand side of your boat when you are facing the bow.

Port light: The red light on the left-hand side of your boat when you face the bow.

Range: The distance an object is from your boat.

Reef knot: A square knot supposedly used for tying in reefs.

Resistance: When a boat is blown through the water, it would prefer not to go. The forces that try to slow the boat are collectively known as its resistance. In light winds the majority of a boat's resistance, or drag, is known as friction drag. That is, the roughness and amount of wetted surface create drag. As the boat's speed increases, wetted-surface drag decreases and wave-making drag increases. At maximum speed the largest portion of the energy holding the boat back is wave-making drag. In other words, the boat is dissipating energy dragging a large wave behind it rather than using this energy to sail faster.

Rhumb line: A line that goes from A to B crossing all meridians at the same angle; or a line that goes from A to B by the shortest distance.

Roller-furling gear: Usually fitted on the headstay, roller-furling gear allows the headsail to be rolled up like a window blind.

Rudder: A movable plate at the back of a boat that is used to control the boat's direction.

Running backstay: An adjustable part of the standing rigging that helps support the mast. Because it can be adjusted, it can be used to bend the mast as well. Sometimes called a runner, or running back.

Sailing school: A place where they teach you all the stuff contained here, usually a cost much higher than this book's.

Sheet: The rope used to pull the sail in.

Shroud: The wire or rod used to hold the mast up in a transverse direction. Shrouds are known as diagonals or verticals. Vertical shrouds go directly up the mast, and diagonals go from the spreader ends or chainplates to the mast.

Singlehanding: What you do when you can't get crew, or don't use your deodorant.

Speed over the ground (SOG): The speed of a boat in relation to the land around or under the boat. If a boat is sailing in a current of two knots that's moving in the same direction as the boat, whose speed is six knots, the vessel's SOG is eight knots. If the current is moving against the boat, the SOG is four knots.

Spinnaker: The large multicolored sail that sailboats set when they are sailing downwind. It's usually set on a pole. The spinnaker pole is adjusted with a guy, and the spinnaker trim is adjusted with a sheet. These are difficult sails to operate and require some practice. Today there are many varieties of spinnaker. A true downwind spinnaker is usually referred to by its weight; for example, the half-ounce lightweight, or 2.2 heavy-weather spinnaker. They are sometimes called chutes, an abbreviated form of parachute spinnaker. (They were originally made from parachute nylon.) For cruising, an MPS (multipurpose spinnaker) or asymmetric spinnaker is often used. Instead of being set on a pole, the spinnaker is fastened at the bow of the boat and tacked or gibed like a normal headsail.

Spreaders: Horizontal struts, usually metal, used to keep the shrouds away from the mast and help support the mast.

Spring tides: The tides that occur when the sun and moon act in conjunction. These are the highest and lowest tides and occur twice every lunar month.

Sprit rig: A four-sided sail supported by a sprit rather than a yard.

Starboard: The right-hand side of your boat when you are facing the bow.

Starboard light: The green light on the right-hand side of your boat.

Steaming light: A light (sometimes called a mastlight) on the forward face of your mast that is turned on when your boat is under power. It should not be used under sail.

Stern light: The white light at the back of your boat.

Tack: To turn the boat through the wind; or the bottom front corner of a sail at the junction of the foot and the luff.

Tacking: Turning the boat so that the wind crosses the bow.

Telltales: Short pieces of wool or tape used to show how the wind is blowing across the sail.

Tidal stream: The tidal current created by a tide rising or falling.

Tide: The rise and fall of the sea according to the phases of the moon. Typically, an area will have two tides per day. When the moon is full, these tides will be higher and lower than normal and are known as spring tides. Neap tides are the opposite, occurring when the rise and fall are at their smallest.

Tiller: The piece of wood fitted to the rudder to steer the boat.

Topping lift: The halyard used to hold the spinnaker pole or bearing-out spar up.

Traveler: If the mainsheet is used to control the tension in the mainsail, the traveler is used to control the angle at which the mainsail is set to the wind. Typically, when sailing in light winds, the boom is located on the centerline. This may mean that the traveler is slightly above centerline.

Trawling: A sailor's term for what happens when the spinnaker or any other sail goes over the side.

Trimaran: A three-hulled sailing vessel. Usually the center hull contains the accommodations, and the two outer hulls (amas) give the boat buoyancy.

True wind: The wind that you would feel if you were standing still on your boat and the boat was not moving.

Turbulence: An area of disturbed wind or water. A tall building creates turbulence on its leeward side.

Upwind: Sailing as close as possible to the wind's direction.

Velocity: A boat's speed.

Velocity made good (VMG): When a boat is sailing to windward, its direct line to its destination is a function of the boat speed and the angle at which the boat is sailing to the wind. If the helmsman pinches up, the boat will slow, but it will also point closer to its destination. If the helmsman reaches off, the boat goes faster but the course to the boat's destination is wider. The combination of these two factors is used to calculate the boat's VMG. Typically, VMG is calculated by onboard wind instruments.

VHF: A radio used aboard boats. Handheld VHF radios have a range of about five to ten miles, while twenty-five-watt console-mounted VHF radios have a range of about twenty-five miles or line of sight. The emergency channel on a VHF radio is channel 16.

Winch: A piece of gear used to improve the mechanical advantage of the crew when hoisting a sail or trimming a sheet.

Wench: A female winch!

Wind shadow: On the leeward side of any object, the wind is turbulent and may be difficult to sail in. Getting downwind of boat or object may put your boat in this area of turbulence, known also as a wind shadow.

INDEX

Gulf Stream, 9
gunkholing, 32
gunwales, 20, 44
gyroscopic compasses, 89, 91

halyards, 20, 21, 64, *66,* 169, 171
harbor traffic, 47
harnesses, 129, 136
hats, 129
header winds, 35–36
headsails, 7, *16,* 51, 151, 153
heaving-to, 158
Heavy Weather Sailing (Coles), 157
Heckard, Scott, 165
helming, 21, 46–49
helmsmen, 7, 36, 48
  crews and, 51
  picking up moorings and, 70
  tacking and, 63
help, calling for, 140–41
high clouds, 144–45, *145–47*
hoisting sail, 29, 62–63
hulls, 4, 7
hurricane holes, 155–56
hydrodynamic forces, 6, *6*
hypothermia, 22, 140–41

IMO (International Maritime Organization), 138
inland waterway buoyage system, 96
Inmarsat telephone system, 139–40
International Convention for the Safety of Life at Sea (SOLAS), 134, 136
International Maritime Organization (IMO), 138

International Rules for Preventing Collisions at Sea (COL-REGS), 109
isobath, 89

jibs, 17, 21, 29
  heaving-to and, 158
  helming and, 49
  hoisting, 64, *65–66,* 66
  trimming of, 51
  wind strength and, 64
jib sheets, *14, 18,* 20, 63
J World (sailing school), 175

keels, 4, 5, 6, 7
  damage from running aground, 105
  lift and, 48
knots (nautical miles per hour), 88
knots (rope), 79–84
  See also specific knots
Kotsch, Rear Admiral, 144

larboard, 46
lateral buoyage system, 96
launch services, 164
leach, 21
leaving a boat, 74–77, *75*
leeboards, 4, 5
"Lee ho," 63
leeward. *See* downwind
life jackets, 1, 3, 22, 129, 133–34, 140
life rafts, 129, 134–35, 142
lift, helming and, 48
lift wind, 35
lights, 94–95, 115–22, *117–21.*
  See also buoys; signals
lockoffs, 170

long-range navigation. *See* loran C

Long Way, The (Moitessier), 157

loran C, 85, 93

Lorrillard, Pierre, 38

lower-level clouds, 147–48

luff, 17, *18,* 64

luff groove, 20

magazines, 40, 41

magnetic compasses, 89–91

mainsail, 8, 17, 20–21, 29, 171
  heaving-to and, 158
  helming and, 49
  setting, 66, *67,* 68, *69*
  trimming, 21, 60

mainsheet, 20, 21, 49

marinas, 25, 29, 121
  leaving boats in, 74–75, *75*
  mooring in, 164

masthead lights, 116, *117,* 118, *118*

masts, 17, 154, 156

Mayday signals, 142

Mercator charts, 86

Micron CSC Extra paint, 173

midchannel buoys, 97

midlevel clouds, 146

mirrors, 137

Moitessier, Bernard, 157

monohulls, 30, 158

mooring lines, 159

moorings
  leaving boats on, 75–76
  leaving from, 60–62, *61–62*
  picking up, 68, 70, *71–72*
  storms and, *154,* 154–55

multihulls, 30–31, *31,* 158

NAMS, 166

National Association of Marine Surveyors (NAMS), 166

National Oceanic and Atmospheric Administration (NOAA), 103

nautical miles, 87, 88

navigation, 85
  basic concepts in, 85–89
  buoyage system in United States, 96, *97, 98,* 98–99
  fixing your position, 91–93
  going aground, 104–6
  planning a trip, 99, *100,* 101–4
  reading the compass, 89–91
  understanding charts, 93–95

New York Yacht Club, 39

night lights, 115–22, *117–21*

NOAA (National Oceanic and Atmospheric Administration), 103

Notice to Mariners, 94

nuns (buoys), 96, *98,* 99

ocean cruising, *33,* 33–34

ocean voyages, 4

off-course movements, 48

offshore (ocean) racing, 38

Offshore Racing Council (ORC), 129, 137

Offshore Sailing School, 175

Optimist dinghies, 3, 17, *17,* 26

ORC (Offshore Racing Council), 129, 137

outriggers, 31